PENGUIN
ARKANA

THE CRYSTAL AND THE WAY OF LIGHT

Born in Degé, Eastern Tibet, in 1938, Namkhai Norbu was recognized at the age of three as the reincarnation of a previous great master of Dzogchen. He then received the full traditional education of a 'Tulku' or reincarnate Lama. Beyond his academic studies, he received teaching from and practised with several great masters in Tibet, before political events made it necessary for him to leave for India. When he was in India, Professor G. Tucci invited him to go to Rome to help with research at the Oriental institute there. He subsequently took up his present post as Professor of Tibetan and Mongolian Language and Literature at the Oriental Institute, University of Naples. In addition to his work at the University, he travels extensively in response to the many requests he receives to give Dzogchen teachings at retreats and seminars all over the world.

John Shane was born in London, and educated there at St Paul's School, and at Emmanuel College, Cambridge. He is a poet, author and musician, who has founded and run a small publishing house, and has worked as a teacher of creative writing. Becoming interested in Buddhism at school, at first through reading Japanese Zen poetry, he later read more widely to include the source material of Indian Buddhism, and the then available material on Tibetan Buddhism. With the arrival of the first Tibetan lamas in Europe he studied and practised under the guidance of a number of them, before meeting Namkhai Norbu Rinpoche soon after the latter began teaching in Europe. He has since travelled widely with Namkhai Norbu to attend his retreats in many parts of the world, including Europe, the United States, India and Nepal, often acting as his translator.

THE CRYSTAL

AND

THE WAY OF LIGHT

SUTRA, TANTRA
AND DZOGCHEN

THE TEACHINGS OF

NAMKHAI NORBU

COMPILED AND EDITED
BY
JOHN SHANE

ARKANA
PENGUIN BOOKS

PENGUIN BOOKS

Published by the Penguin Group
Penguin Books Ltd, 27 Wrights Lane, London W8 5TZ, England
Penguin Books USA Inc., 375 Hudson Street, New York, New York 10014, USA
Penguin Books Australia Ltd, Ringwood, Victoria, Australia
Penguin Books Canada Ltd, 10 Alcorn Avenue, Toronto, Ontario, Canada M4V 3B2
Penguin Books (NZ) Ltd, 182–190 Wairau Road, Auckland 10, New Zealand

Penguin Books Ltd, Registered Offices: Harmondsworth, Middlesex, England

First published by Routledge & Kegan Paul Ltd 1986
Published by Arkana 1993
10 9 8 7 6 5 4 3 2

Made and printed in Great Britain by
Clays Ltd, St Ives plc

This book is dedicated to my master
  Jyăñqub Dórjé,
  to my uncles
Urgyán Danzìn and Kyèntse Qosgi Wáñqyug,
and to the benefit of all sentient beings.

Namkhai Norbu

Contents

Illustrations

Nāmo Guru Bhy!
Nāmo Ḍeva Bhy!
Nāmo Ḍākinī Bhy!

Just as the sun rises in the sky, so, too, may the Great Secret Treasure of all the Victorious Ones, the supreme Zógqen teaching, arise and spread in all realms!

(At the top of the page, the white Tibetan letter 'A', symbol of the primordial state of the mind; below it, salutation to the Three Roots, Guru, Ḍeva, and Ḍākinī; and finally the words of Padmsambhava's homage to the Zógqen teachings. The 'Victorious Ones' referred to are those who have overcome the dualistic condition.)

Editor's note

This book has been compiled from the transcripts of tapes of oral teachings given by Namkhai Norbu Rinpoche at retreats and lectures in various parts of the world during the last seven years, as well as from my own notes from untaped or untranscribed lectures, and from material arising from private conversations with Rinpoche.

Although Rinpoche has a good knowledge of English, he has preferred (until late 1984) to teach in Italian, the Western language with which he is most familiar. He pauses every few sentences to allow for translation into the language of the majority of his listeners, or, when in Italy, to allow for translation into English for those present who do not understand Italian. This book could not, then, have been produced without the dedicated effort of all those who have translated, recorded, and transcribed Rinpoche's teachings, but although the spontaneous translation is often inspired, when transcribed verbatim the result leaves much to be desired on the printed page.

One of the principal tasks of the Editor has, then, been to render all the material used into good written English. But over and above that, from the many transcripts dealing in detail with different topics, an overall form for the book had to be devised that would bring out the inherent structure of teachings as a whole, without losing the very distinctive quality of Rinpoche's oral teaching style. I have attempted to do this by keeping to the pattern of alternating between the teachings themselves and Rinpoche's entertaining and illuminating stories that so effectively illustrate the teachings. Since the book is aimed at the general, as well as the scholarly, reader, I have tried as much as possible to avoid weighting the text down with notes.

If I have to any extent succeeded in my work as Editor, it is due to the patience of Namkhai Norbu Rinpoche himself, in continually making time available in private for further explanation and clarification. However, any errors, or wrong emphasis that may remain in the text are entirely my own responsibility.

Too many friends have helped in this project to mention them all by name, but I would particularly like to thank my wife, Jo, for her unfailing support and encouragement.

At this time of pressing crisis for humanity, it is of the utmost importance that the ancient traditions of wisdom that lead to the transformation of the individual should be preserved and communicated clearly, as they have such a great contribution to offer to that peaceful transformation of society upon which the future survival of our species and our planet now depends. I hope that the collaboration with Namkhai Norbu Rinpoche on this book, which it has been my great privilege to enjoy, will truly serve to play some part, however small, in the great endeavour of bringing strife and discord to an end, and in furthering peace and freedom from suffering for all beings.

The reader is asked to remember that no book can ever be a substitute for receiving transmission from a qualified master. May those who do not already have such a true 'spiritual friend' be fortunate enough to find one!

May it be auspicious!

John Shane
Arcidosso, June 1985

The Six Vajra Verses

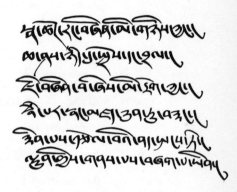

Although apparent phenomena
manifest as diversity
  yet this diversity is non-dual,
  and of all the multiplicity
  of individual things that exist
none can be confined in a limited concept.

Staying free from the trap of any attempt
to say 'it's like this', or 'like that',
it becomes clear that all manifested forms are
aspects of the infinite formless,
  and, indivisible from it,
  are self-perfected.

Seeing that everything is self-perfected
  from the very beginning,
the disease of striving for any achievement
  is surrendered,
and just remaining in the natural state
  as it is,
the presence of non-dual contemplation
continuously spontaneously arises.

Note to the Six Vajra Verses

The Six Vajra Verses, or more literally, the 'Six Vajra Lines', since the original Tibetan consists of only six lines, contain a perfect résumé of the Zógqen teachings. This translation is by Brian Beresford and John Shane, in a fairly free rendering following the oral explanation of Namkhai Norbu. The illustration shows the Six Verses in Tibetan cursive Wúmed script; calligraphy by Namkhai Norbu. The whole of the main text section of this book could be considered to be a commentary on these Six Verses, which are the content of the Draxisbai Pal Rigbai Kujyug Tantra, the 'Fortune Bringing Cuckoo of Non-dual Awareness (rigba) Tantra'. As the cuckoo is the first herald of coming Spring, so this Tantra and these Verses are the heralds of coming spiritual awakening.

Guide to pronunciation of Tibetan names and terms

Tibetan names and terms have been transcribed according to a system devised by Namkhai Norbu.

This system is based on phonetic transcription rather than a transliteration, and is very similar to the generally accepted Pinyin system for the transcription of the Chinese language, with which many scholars are already familiar.

1 This symbol ˇ indicates a low tone.
2 This symbol ˋ indicates a nasalization before the immediately following consonant (as in ingot).
3 This symbol ´ indicates a stress in the pronunciation.

Tibetan spelling		English sound	Tibetan spelling		English sound
Ca	—	*k*arma	Bă	—	*p*ath, low tone
Că	—	*k*arma, low tone	Bà	—	am*b*er, nasalized
			Bá	—	*b*anner, stressed
Gà	—	si*ng*able, nasalized			
Gá	—	*g*ale, stressed	Sa	—	*s*and
			Să	—	*s*and, low tone
Ja	—	*ch*ant	Sà	—	*s*and, as usual
Jă	—	*ch*ant, low tone	Sá	—	*s*and, stressed
Jà	—	a*ng*el, nasalized			
Já	—	*j*ade, stressed	Xa	—	*sh*ore
			Xă	—	*sh*ore, low tone
Da	—	*t*antra	Xà	—	*sh*ore, stressed
Dă	—	*t*antra, low tone	Xá	—	*j*our
Dà	—	stan*d*ard, nasalized			
Dá	—	*d*ay, stressed	Za	—	ca*ts*
			Ză	—	wor*ds*
Ba	—	*p*ath			

xvii

Tibetan spelling	English sound
Zà	— words, nasalized
Zá	— words, stressed
Na	— nine
Nà	— nine, nasalized
Ná	— nine, stressed
Ña	— ring
Ñà	— ring, nasalized
Ñá	— ring, stressed
Ña	— new
Ñà	— new, nasalized
Ñá	— new, stressed
Ma	— man
Mà	— man, nasalized
Má	— man, stressed
Ka	— aspirated union of k+h
Kà	— as above, preceded by nasalization, nkha
Qa	— channel, with strongly aspirated h
Qà	— channel, preceded by nasalization
Ta	— aspirated, t-ha
Tà	— nasalized, nt-ha
Pa	— aspirated, p-ha
Pà	— nasalized, np-ha
Ca	— ts-ha
Cà	— nasalized, nts-ha
Ya	— yes
Yá	— yes, stressed
ra	— rainbow
Rá	— rainbow, stressed
La	— light
Lá	— light, nasalized
Wa	— water
Wá	— water, stressed

Tibetan spelling	English sound
Va	— water, low tone
Ha	— hut
Hã	— soundless h, vowel in low tone
Gya	— kiosk
Gyă	— kiosk, low tone
Gyà	— gya, preceded by nasalization, nghya
Gyá	— gya, stressed
Jya	— chya, non-aspirated
Jyă	— chya, low tone
Jyà	— jya, preceded by nasalization, njya
Jyá	— jya, stressed
Kya	— k aspirated+y, khya
Kyà	— aspirated, nkhya
Qya	— cha, aspirated
Qyà	— ncha, nasalized
Dra	— translation
Dră	— translation, low tone
Drà	— translation, preceded by nasalization, ntra
Drá	— translation, stressed
Tra	— t-hra
Trà	— nt-hra
Lha	— hla
Hra	— sHra

Vowels

A	— allah
I	— me
U	— moon
E	— way
O	— ore

Final consonants
preceded by a vowel

-g — back
-ṅ — ring
-b — trip (lightly)
-m — hum
-s — soundless, changes the
        preceding vowel
  1 as as e in met
  2 is as e in me
  3 us as German ü
  4 es as é in René

Final consonants
preceded by a vowel

  5 o as German ö
-d — cat, vowels change
        as with -s
-n — pen, vowels change
        as with -s
-r — car (lightly, the
        vowel lengthens)
-l — fill, vowels change
        as with -s

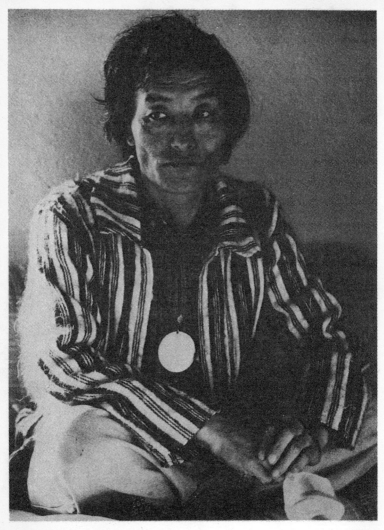

Namkhai Norbu Rinpoche, in Italy, 1979, wearing round his neck a 'meloṅ', or mirror, made of five precious metals, a symbol used in explaining the Zógqen teachings. (Photo: Jill Purce)

CHAPTER 1

My birth, early life and education; and how I came to meet my principal master

From the very beginning
all the infinite number of beings that exist
have as their essential inherent condition
the perfectly pure state of an enlightened being;
knowing this to be true also of me,
I commit myself to supreme realization.

Lines on Bodhicitta, written by Lóñqenba (1308–63), expressing the concept of the Base in the Anu Yoga

When I was born, in the village of Géug, in the Goñra district of Dégé, eastern Tibet, on the seventeenth day of the tenth month of the year of the Earth Tiger (8 December 1938), it is said that the rose trees outside my parents' house bloomed even though it was winter. Two of my uncles came at once to visit my family. They had been disciples of

An eighteenth century crystal polyhedron from Tibet (John Dugger and David Medalla, London)

a certain great master, Azòm Drùgba, who had died some years before, and they were both now Zógqen masters themselves. They firmly believed that I was a reincarnation of their master, both because of things that he had said to them before he died, and because he had bequeathed certain special possessions to a son who he said would be born to my parents after his death. When I was two years old I was officially recognized as a reincarnation by a high drulgu (tulku) of the Nínmaba school,[1] who made me a gift of some robes. I don't remember many of the details of what happened then, but I do know that after that I received an awful lot of presents!

Later, at the age of five, I was also recognized by the sixteenth Garmaba and by the Sidu Rinboqe (Situ Rinpoche) of that time as the mind incarnation of another great master, who was in turn the reincarnation of the founder of the modern state of Bhutan, and whose lineage had been the Dharmarajas, or temporal and spiritual rulers of that state up until the early twentieth century. As I grew up I was thus to be given quite a few names and titles, many of which are very long and grand sounding. But I have never used them, because I have always preferred the name my parents gave me at birth. They called me Namkhai Norbu, which is rather a special name in its own way. Norbu means jewel, and Namkhai means of the sky, or of space. It's unusual for the genitive to be used in Tibetan names, but that's what my parents chose to call me because, although they had four fine daughters, they had been longing for years to have a son. So strong had been this longing, in fact, that they had engaged the services of a monk to perform an invocation of Tārā [see illustration and note on p. 4] on their behalf for a whole year, asking for the granting of their wish. This monk also became my sisters' tutor. Eventually he had a dream which he interpreted as a favourable sign. He dreamed that a beautiful plant grew up right in front of the hearth of my parents' home. The plant put forth a beautiful yellow flower that opened and grew very big. The monk was sure that this indicated the birth of a male child. Later, when I was born, my parents' were so happy that they felt I was a gift from the heavens. So they called me 'Jewel of Space', and that is the name I have always stuck to.

My parents were always very kind to me, and I grew up into a little boy as mischievous as any other, and learned to read and write at home. As a young child I often dreamed I was travelling at great speed inside what seemed to me to be a tiger, a strange roaring beast. I had never seen a motor vehicle, as there were none at that time in our part of Tibet. Later, of course, I came to travel in many cars, and then I recognized them as being what I had seen in my dreams. When, as a teenager, I did catch my first sight of a lorry, I was on horseback on a mountainside at night looking down at the vehicles passing on the new Chinese road below. The tail lights glowed red on the giant trucks thundering by, and I thought they must be on fire. I also dreamed of strange flaming flying objects that exploded causing terrible destruction. I now know that what I saw were the missiles that were being developed far away in other parts of the world, but fortunately I have never yet seen in waking life the war I saw then as a child in my dream.

I sometimes played such pranks on our neighbours that I would be in serious trouble when my father came home from the travels that his work often involved. He would beat me, and I would be very angry, and try to get my own back on the neighbours who had told my father what I had done by playing even more pranks on them. Then, of course, I would be in more trouble again. I began to become more considerate largely as a result of my grandmother's influence. She had been a disciple of Azòm Drùgba, and she took a great interest in me. She sometimes managed to keep me from being punished by preventing my parents finding out what I had done. I remember that I once found the dead body of a large rodent called a marmot. Unnoticed by anyone I spent a blissful afternoon playing with the dead creature,

Green Tārā   There are twenty-one different Sambhogakaya
manifestations of Tārā, a feminine emanation of the
primordial Dharmakāya Buddha Amitābha. Each form of
Tārā embodies a particular aspect of compassion. Green
Tārā represents the active, energic aspect of compassion,
and she is the national protectress of Tibet, while White
Tārā, for example, embodies the fertile, motherly aspect
of compassion.

4

even filling the body up with water and whirling it round my head. But when I took my plaything to bed with me my grandmother noticed it. She knew that my mother would have been very upset if she had known what I had been doing, and would have worried that I might become infected with some disease, so my grandmother didn't tell anyone. I thought this was very kind of her, and in fact I loved her very much. So when I saw her quietly weeping to herself about my behaviour when she thought I was asleep, I was deeply moved, and resolved to mend my ways. But I can't say that I ever completely succeeded in overcoming my mischievousness altogether.

When I was five years old I was playing outside our house one day when twelve monks arrived, all very elegantly dressed. The place where we lived was very isolated, and hardly any travellers ever passed, so I was very surprised to see them. I couldn't think why they had come. They went into the house, and a little later I was called to go in after them. I was taken into the small shrine room we had there, and they dressed me in fine silk robes. I didn't understand why I was being dressed up, but I enjoyed it just the same. I sat there, on a high throne they had specially prepared for me, for hours and hours while they performed a ritual, and then they went away. I thought to myself: 'Well, that's the end of that.' But everyone went on reminding me that I was a reincarnation and showing me great respect, and I soon realized that far from being the end of anything, everything was just beginning.

A couple of weeks later some monks came and took me to Dégé Gónqen monastery, which was a very important place in that region: the King of Dégé himself lived there. My father worked in the King's administration, at first as an official roughly equivalent to a mayor or provincial governor in the West, and later, since he loved animals so much, as the head of a department whose function was to prevent hunting out of season or in excess in the whole of that part of Tibet. I was taken in to see the King, and since I was now recognized as a reincarnation, he made me a gift of an entire building inside the monastery compound. I lived there until I was nine years old with a master, a teacher who made me study hard day and night. There were many things to learn, including all the rules and prayers of the monastery. A monk normally finishes at nineteen years of age the phase of study I undertook there. But I completed it at the age of eight, because my master was so strict, and I was allowed no free time at all. I also had a natural gift for memorizing things. My mischievous side did manage to surface from time to time, however. I remember, for example, that once, when the King was involved in a military ceremony that required him to sit still on horseback for some time in the courtyard below and opposite the first floor window of my house, I leaned over the sill and used a mirror to reflect the sun's rays into his eyes and dazzle him, in order to distract him from the somewhat heavy seriousness of the occasion. Fortunately for me, the King knew me very well by that time, and he even enjoyed the joke himself, when he had recovered his composure.

Then for a year I learned all the rules for the drawing and practice of maṇḍala, after which I went away to monastic college. A college always has its rules, and the rule of the one I attended was that one studied there for five years. But since I entered at a much earlier age than usual, I was there six years. I was only nine years old, and the normal age of entry was at least thirteen. So they didn't count my first year which was regarded as a sort of test to see if I was capable of staying the course. It wasn't just a matter of memorizing things any longer: we studied philosophy, which requires a capacity to reason well, and many people found the going too tough and dropped out. Life in the college was certainly not always easy for me either, at such a young age, and I suffered as others do from the rigours of life in that kind of institution. I had to learn some very practical lessons very quickly. When my father left me at the college for my first term, he left with me sufficient supplies for the whole three months of that term. But I had never had to manage my own resources by myself before, and I used up all my supplies about half way through the period they were supposed to last, because I was far too generous in my hospitality to all my new colleagues. When I had no food left of my own, I managed to survive for about a week on the tea that was the only thing provided by the college, before I could face the humiliation of having to go and ask my teacher for assistance. He arranged for me to receive a bowl of soup every evening. The next term I was a good deal more provident with my resources.

The regulations there were very strict, and we had to be in our small rooms every night to practise and study. Butter lamps and coal for heating were supplied, but not in generous quantities, and I remember that once my lamp ran out before I had completed the large number of practices I had to read through every night to maintain the commitments I had made in receiving the very many initiations given to a drulgu like myself. We were not permitted to leave our rooms at that hour, and there was a monk who patrolled the corridors to enforce compliance with the rules, so I didn't dare go to ask a neighbour if I could borrow a lamp. I tried to read my practices by the light of the coal fire, and some of them I knew well enough to manage to recite even when the embers had burned right down to a mere glimmer. But finally the last spark went out, and there I was in the dark with a pile of long Tibetan pages still to be read if I was to maintain my samaya commitment. I didn't understand at that time how to maintain commitment by applying the essentials of practice, and I interpreted and carried out all my instructions very literally.

In my holidays I found time to visit my two uncles, and those visits were very important to me, because they were both great practitioners of Zógqen. I shall tell some stories of my experiences with these uncles, the one an abbot and the other a yogi, at intervals in the explanations of the teachings that follow in the later chapters of this book. My relationships with them were of very great importance to me throughout my college years, and as practitioners they were a vital counterbalance to the intellectual studies that took up most of my time from the age of nine to the age of sixteen. In 1954, at the age of sixteen, I completed my studies and left college. I knew a great deal about all the forms of the teaching, and had studied Tibetan medicine and astrology. I could recite whole texts of philosophy and ritual by heart. I had studied diligently with many masters, and had even been called upon to teach certain subjects in college. It seemed to me then that I understood them well enough, but as I came to realize later, I had not really understood anything at all.

Though I did not yet know it, events were moving me towards the one particular master who was to bring all I had learned and experienced into a new and more profound perspective, and through contact with whom I was to come to a re-awakening, and to a true understanding of the Zógqen teachings. Through his inspiration I came to know the importance of these teachings, and eventually to teach them myself in the Western world. This master was not a grand personage. Tibetans in general are used to famous teachers of high rank, who present themselves in grand style. Without such outer signs people cannot usually recognize the qualities of a master, and I myself might have been no different. But, on leaving college, I was given my first official responsibilities, and was sent to China as a representative of Tibetan youth at the Provincial Assembly of the Province of Szechuan, the local governing body. While I was there I began learning the Chinese language, and also taught Tibetan, so with these activities as well as my official function I was very busy. But I could not avoid noticing the very different social and political structure there, and wondering how what was happening in China would finally affect my own country and its people. Then one night I had a dream. In this dream, I saw a place with many white houses, built of cement. As this is not a Tibetan style of building, but is a style common in China, I mistakenly (as I later learned) assumed that these houses were Chinese. But when, still dreaming, I went closer, I saw that on one of them the mantra of Padmasambhava was written in very large Tibetan script. I was amazed, because if this was a Chinese house, why would there be a mantra written in Tibetan over the door? I opened the door, went in, and inside saw an old man; just a seemingly normal old man. I thought to myself: 'Is it possible that this man is really a master?' But then he bent to touch his forehead to mine in the way that Tibetan masters give blessings, and began to recite the mantra of Padmasambhava. All this still seemed very surprising to me, but I was now fully convinced that he was a master. Then the old man told me to go round to the other side of a large rock that was nearby, and said that in the middle of the rock I would find a cave containing eight natural maṇḍalas. He said that I should go there at once to look at them. What he said amazed me even more, but I nevertheless went right away. When I got to the cave, my father appeared behind me, and as I went in he began to recite the Prajñāpāramitā sūtra, an important Mahāyāna sūtra, in a loud voice. I began to recite the sūtra along with him, and together we walked all around inside the cave. I couldn't see all of the eight maṇḍalas, only the corners and edges of them, but with their presence in my mind I awoke.

A year after this dream, when I had returned to Tibet, a man came to visit my father in our village, and I overheard him telling my father about a very extraordinary doctor whom he had just met. He described the place where the doctor lived, and he described the man in detail, and as he spoke the memory of my dream returned to me. I felt sure that the man he was describing was the same man I had seen in it. I spoke to my father, to whom I had told the dream shortly after it occurred, and reminding him of the dream, asked him if we could visit this doctor. My father agreed, and we left the next day. We had to journey for four days on horseback, but when we got there, the old man I met really seemed to be the one I had seen in my dream. I really had the sense that I had been in that village before, with its Tibetan houses made in Chinese style concrete, and the mantra over the old man's door. So I had no doubt that he was to be my master, and I remained there to receive teaching from him. This teacher's name was Jyăñqub Dórjé (Chanchub Dórjé), and in terms of outward appearances he seemed like a normal country person of Tibet. His style of dress, and his way of life were just ordinary on the surface, though in this book I shall relate some further stories of him that show that his state of being was far from ordinary. Around him his disciples also lived in a very ordinary way, most of them being very simple people, not at all well-to-do, who grew and tended crops, working on the land and practising together.

Jyăñqub Dórjé was a Zógqen master, and Zógqen does not depend on externals; rather it is a teaching about the essentials of the human condition. Thus, when I later left Tibet because of the political difficulties there and finally settled in the West to take up a post as a Professor at the Oriental Institute of the University of Naples, Italy, I came to see that though the outer conditions and culture in which people lived were different to those I had left behind in Tibet, the fundamental condition of every individual was no different. I saw that since the Zógqen teachings are not dependent on culture, they can be taught, understood, and practised in any cultural context.

CHAPTER 2

An introductory perspective: the Zógqen teachings and the culture of Tibet

> If you give an explanation of Zógqen
> to 100 people who are interested,
> this is not enough;
> but if you give an explanation
> to one person who is not interested,
> this is too much.
>
> Gárab Dórjé

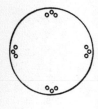

Many people today are not interested at all in spiritual matters, and their lack of interest is reinforced by the generally materialistic outlook of our society. If you ask them what they believe in, they may even say that they don't believe in anything. Such people think that all religion is based on faith, which they regard as little better than superstition, with no relevance to the modern world. But Zógqen cannot be regarded as a religion, and does not ask anyone to believe in anything. Rather, it suggests that the individual observe him or herself, and discover what their actual condition is.

In the Zógqen teachings, the individual is regarded as functioning at three interdependent levels, of body, voice or energy, and mind. Even someone who says they don't believe in anything cannot say they don't believe in their own body! It's basic to their existence, and the limits and problems of the body are clearly tangible. We feel cold and hunger, we suffer pain and loneliness, and we spend much of our lives in an attempt to overcome our physical suffering.

The level of energy, or voice, is not so easy to see, and not so widely understood. Even medical

11

doctors in the West are largely ignorant of it, trying to cure all illnesses at a purely physical level. But if the energy of an individual is disturbed, neither the body nor the mind of the individual will be well balanced. Certain illnesses, such as cancer, are caused by disturbances of the energy, and cannot be cured simply by surgery or medication. Similarly, many mental illnesses, and also some less severe mental problems, are caused by poor circulation of energy. Our minds are generally very complicated and confused, and even when we want to stay calm, we may find we can't, because our nervous and agitated energy won't allow us to. So to deal with these problems of body, voice and mind, the Zógqen teachings present practices that work with each of these three levels of the individual, practices that can be integrated with the individual's daily life and which can thus change our whole life experience from one of tension and confusion to one of wisdom and true freedom. The teachings are not merely theoretical, they are practical; and though the Zógqen teachings are extremely ancient, because the nature of the body, voice and mind of the individual has not changed, these teachings remain as relevant to the human situation of today as they were to that of yesterday.

The primordial state

The teaching of Zógqen is in essence a teaching concerning the primordial state of being that is each individual's own intrinsic nature from the very beginning. To enter this state is to experience oneself as one is, as the centre of the universe – though not in the ordinary ego sense. The ordinary ego-centred consciousness is precisely the limited cage of dualistic vision that closes off the experience of one's own true nature, which is the space of the primordial state. To understand this primordial state is to understand the teaching of Zógqen, and the function of the transmission of the teaching of

Zógqen is to communicate this state, from one who has realized it, or made real that which was previously only latent, to those who remain caught up in the dualistic condition. Even the name 'Zógqen', which means 'Great Perfection', refers to the self-perfectedness of this state, fundamentally pure from the beginning, with nothing to reject or accept.

To understand and enter the primordial state one does not need intellectual, cultural, or historical knowledge. It is beyond intellect by its very nature. Yet when people hear of a teaching they have not heard of before, one of the first things they may want to know is where this teaching arose, where it came from, who taught it, and so on. This is understandable, but Zógqen itself cannot be said to belong to the culture of any country. There is a tantra of Zógqen, the 'Drá Talgùr Zavai Gyúd', for example, that says that the Zógqen teaching can be found in thirteen solar systems other than our own, so we can't even truly say that the Zógqen teaching belongs to this planet Earth, much less to any particular national culture. Although it is true that the tradition of Zógqen that we are about to consider has been transmitted through the culture of Tibet that has harboured it ever since the beginning of recorded history in Tibet, we nevertheless cannot finally say that Zógqen is Tibetan, because the primordial state itself has no nationality, and is omnipresent, everywhere.

But it is also true that beings everywhere have entered into the dualistic vision that blocks the experience of the primordial state. And when realized beings have tried to communicate with them, they have only rarely been able to communicate the primordial state completely without words or symbols, so they have made use of whatever culture they found present, as a means of communication. In this way it has often happened that the culture and the teachings have become interwoven, and in the case of Tibet this is true to the extent that it is not possible to understand the culture without an understanding of the teachings.

It is not that the teachings of Zógqen were ever

particularly widespread or well-known in Tibet; in fact rather the reverse was true. Zógqen was always a somewhat reserved teaching. But the Zógqen teachings are the essence of all Tibetan teachings, so direct that they were always kept a little hidden, and people were often a little afraid of them. Furthermore, there existed a tradition of Zógqen among the ancient Bön[1] traditions, the indigenous shamanic traditions of Tibet, that pre-date the arrival of Buddhism from India. Thus, if we consider the Zógqen teachings as being the essence of all the Tibetan spiritual traditions, both Buddhist and Bön (though itself actually belonging to neither Buddhism nor Bön), and if we understand that the spiritual traditions of Tibet were the essence of Tibetan culture, then we can use the Zógqen teachings as a key to the understanding of Tibetan culture as a whole. And with this perspective it can be seen how all the various aspects of Tibetan culture have been manifested as facets of the unified vision of realized beings, the masters of the spiritual traditions.

Like a crystal at the heart of the culture, the clarity of the primordial state, as manifested in the minds of many masters, has thrown out the forms of Tibetan art and iconography, medicine and astrology, like brilliant rays, or sparkling reflections. So by coming to understand the nature of the crystal, we will be better able to make sense of the rays and reflections that emanate from it.

CHAPTER 3

How my master Jyăñqub Dórjé showed me the real meaning of Direct Introduction

Knowledge of Zógqen
is like being on the highest
mountain peak;
no level of mountain remains
mysterious or hidden,
and whoever finds themselves
on this highest peak
cannot be conditioned
by anyone or anything.

From a tantra of the
Zógqen Upadeṣa

When I went to my master Jyăñqub Dórjé I was educated up to the hilt in the intellectual sense. My mind was filled with everything I'd learned in the monastic colleges. I thought that to receive transmission of the teachings, elaborate ritual initiations were essential, and I asked Jyăñqub Dórjé to give me a certain initiation. I asked him every day for days and days, but he always refused. 'What's the use?', he'd say. 'You've already received so many of those initiations from your other masters; initiations like that are not the principle of the Zógqen teachings. Transmission isn't only received in formal initiations.' But no matter what he said, I remained fixed on the kind of perfectly performed ritual initiations other masters had always given me. I wasn't satisfied with his replies, and I wanted him to put on a special hat, prepare a maṇḍala, and pour a little water on my head, or something like that. That was what I really, sincerely wanted; but he always continued to refuse.

Finally I insisted so much that he at last agreed. He promised that about two months later, on the day of Padmasambhava, the tenth day of the Tibetan lunar month,[1] he would give me the initiation I wanted, the empowerment of Samantabhadra and the peaceful and wrathful divinities of the Bărdo.[2] This initiation is actually not very complicated, and a master skilled in such things could have completed it very quickly. But Jyăñqub Dórjé had never received a formal education, and he was not used to giving initiations. When the long awaited day finally came, the initiation took him from about nine in the morning till midnight! To begin with, he had to prepare himself by performing a rite of self-initiation. This took him until mid-day to complete. Then he began the initiation for me. But firstly, not being formally educated, he couldn't read the text, and then on top of that I saw that he didn't know how to do all the ritual things he was supposed to do. He wasn't that kind of a master. So he had a disciple present as an assistant who was himself an expert teacher, and he prepared all the maṇḍalas and ritual objects. Then the disciple began to read the text to tell the master what he had to do next. But when he read out that the master should do a certain mudrā, or gesture, Jyăñqub Dórjé didn't know how to do it, so they had to stop while he learned it. Then there was a whole long invocation that was supposed to be chanted, invoking all the masters of the lineage, and while chanting it, the master is supposed to sound a bell and a ḍamaru, or small drum. Someone who is used to rituals can perform all this very quickly, but Jyăñqub Dórjé wasn't used to such things, and the whole situation became outrageous, a complete farce. First of all he worked out with his assistant what was written in the notes to the text. 'Ah!', he said, 'It says here that you have to sound the bell!' So he took the bell, and for about five minutes all he did was sound it over and over again. Then he read that you have to sound the ḍamaru [see p. 48]. So he sounded the little drum over and over for about another five minutes. Then he suddenly said: 'Oh,

16

now I see! You have to sound the bell and ḍamaru together!', so he did that. But by then he had forgotten what it was that he was supposed to chant, so he had to go through it all again with the help of the disciple who could read. Jyăñqub Dórjé himself hadn't had the kind of education that involves study, but was a practitioner who, through the development of his practice, had manifested wisdom and clarity, and was thus a master. So he stumbled through the initiation taking all day and a good deal of the evening to do it. By the time he had finished I was almost in a state of shock, as I knew very well how an initiation should be done, and it was nothing like this.

But by then it was nearly midnight, and we were all very hungry. We sang the Song of the Vajra [see p. 58] together many times, a short, slow, anthemic chant that leads the practitioner into contemplation through integration with its actual sound, its syllabic structure ensuring deepeningly relaxed breathing. This is characteristic of the way Zógqen works with ritual. Then we recited a short Gana Puja offering, and ate. After the meal the master gave me a real explanation of the true meaning of initiation and transmission, and I realized that despite all the formal initiations I had received, I had never understood or entered into the true meaning of them.

Then, without interruption, for about three or four hours, Jyăñqub Dórjé gave me a real explanation of Zógqen, not teaching me in an intellectual style, but in a very straightforward and relaxed, friendly conversational way. Despite all my education, this was the first time a master had really made such a direct attempt to get me to understand something. What he said, and the way that he said it, was exactly like a tantra of Zógqen, spoken spontaneously, continuously aloud. I knew that even a very learned scholar would not be able to speak like that. He was speaking from clarity and not just from an intellectual understanding. From that day on I understood that intellectual study, which had always previously been so important to me, is only of secondary value. And I understood

Xènrab Miwo

གེ༷ན་རབ་མི་བོ་ཀུན་ལས་རྣམ་པར་རྒྱལ་བ

Tibetan wood-block print of Xènrab Miwo, seated on a lotus throne, holding a swastika sceptre, Bŏn equivalent of the Buddhist vajra, symbol of the indestructible, eternal nature of primordial energy.

The earliest available historical records relate that a great Bŏn spiritual master, Xènrab Miwo, born in 1856 B.C., reformed and synthesized the various existing Bŏn traditions, replacing actual animal sacrifices with the use of ritual statuettes, and introducing the earliest known form of Zógqen teaching (Yañdagbai Sembŏn), a form less sophisticated than the Three Series of Gárab Dórjé.

18

that the principle of transmission is not just the performance of rituals or initiations, or the giving of intellectual explanations. That day my mental constructions completely collapsed. Up until then I was completely boxed in with all the ideas I had received in my college education.

Transmission is vital to the Introduction received in Zógqen, and the Direct Introduction I received from Jyăñqub Dórjé that day, and continued to receive throughout my stay with him, was typical of the way in which transmission of the Zógqen teachings has been passed on down the lineage from master to disciple, from the time of Gárab Dórjé, the first master of Zógqen, who himself received transmission through direct visionary contact with the Sambhogakāya [see p. 130].

Although a simpler and less sophisticated form of the Zógqen teachings had been introduced into the many streams of the Bŏn tradition by Xènrab Miwo [see p. 18], the great reformer of Bŏn, many years before the time of Gárab Dórjé, nevertheless what we now know as the Three Series of the Zógqen teachings were taught for the first time on this planet in this time cycle by Gárab Dórjé. And although the great master Padmasambhava, who came later, is undoubtedly more widely known, it was from Gárab Dórjé that he received transmission, both directly, in the form of a visionary transmission across time and space, and, in the usual way, as the teachings had descended down

---

The root of the word 'Bŏn' means 'to recite', or 'chant', and so this name was applied to all those who recited mantras, or performed rituals. Historically, one cannot properly speak of a single 'Bŏn religion', but only of a confluence of many streams of shamanic tradition. The fact that there is an etymological link between the word 'Bŏn' and the Tibetan word for Tibet, 'Bŏd', shows how deeply these traditions were identified with the area, and rooted in it. Bŏn ritual practices work to enable the individual to go beyond dualism, and to master the functioning of energy.

the lineage of Gárab Dórjé's disciples and their disciples in turn.

Gárab Dórjé was a totally realized being who manifested a birth in a Nirmāṇakāya form [see p. 130], as a human being, in about 184 BC., in the country of Urgyán, which was situated to the north west of India. He spent his life there teaching to both human beings and the Ḍākinīs [see p. 2 of commentary to plate section]. His final teaching before he entered the Body of Light, was to summarize the teachings in Three Principles, sometimes known as 'The Three Last Testaments of Gárab Dórjé'.

The life of Gárab Dórjé

Gárab Dórjé, unlike Buddha Šākyamuni who lived before his time, but like Padmasambhava who was to come later, did not manifest an ordinary birth. A realized being can choose the manner, time and place of his or her birth in a way that seems impossible from the limited point of view of dualistic vision. Gárab Dórjé's mother, Sudharma, was the daughter of the King of Urgyán, and she was a nun. The child she bore was conceived after a meditative vision, an event that both delighted and baffled her. She was ashamed, and afraid that people would think badly of her or believe that the child was a phantom because he had been born to a virgin, she hid him in a cinder pit. When, a few days later, she returned full of remorse, she found the child radiantly healthy and playing in the ashes. From then on it was accepted that the child was a miraculous incarnation of a great teacher, and he was brought up in the King's palace. Spontaneously and untaught, he began to recite essential tantras as if from memory, out of his great clarity, and the King found such joy in his company that he named him 'Praharsha Vajra', which means 'Joyous Vajra' in the language of Urgyán, a language similar to Sanskrit. In Tibetan that name becomes 'Gárab Dórjé'.

20

Gárab Dórjé
(Line drawing
by Nigel Wellings.)

Gárab Dórjé's
three principles
of the Zógqen
teaching

1   *DIRECT INTRODUCTION* to the primordial state is transmitted straight away by the master to the disciple. The master always remains in the primordial state, and the presence of the state communicates itself to the disciple in whatever situation or activity they may share.

2   *THE DISCIPLE* enters into non-dual contemplation and, experiencing the primordial state, *NO LONGER REMAINS IN ANY DOUBT* as to what it is.

3   *THE DISCIPLE CONTINUES IN THE STATE* of non-dual contemplation, the primordial state, bringing contemplation into every action, until that which is every individual's true condition from the beginning (the Dharmakāya, see p. 130), but which remains obscured by dualistic vision, is made real, or realized. One continues right up to Total Realization (p. 131).

At the age of seven, when all the learned pandits of the kingdom were gathered in debate, Gárab Dórjé defeated them in argument, showing far greater understanding than any of them. He then taught them the Zógqen teachings, and the news spread rapidly far afield that a young boy considered to be the reincarnation of a great being, living in the country of Urgyán, was giving a teaching beyond the law of cause and effect.

When the news reached India it greatly disturbed the Buddhist pandits there, and it was decided that the most learned pandit of all, whose name was Mañjushrimitra, who was extremely skilled in logic and argument, should lead a party to defeat this impudent young upstart in debate. But when Mañjuṣrimitra arrived he found that the boy was indeed a great teacher, and that he could not fault his teaching. It became clear to him that the child's realization went well beyond his own intellectual understanding. He then became deeply repentant, and confessed to Gárab Dórjé the wrong motivation he had had in coming to see him with the sole intention of debating with him and defeating him in argument. Gárab Dórjé forgave him, and proceeded to give him more teaching. What he did ask of Mañjuṣrimitra, however, was that he, the greatest of all the Buddhist scholars of his time, should write a text setting out the argument of the teaching with which Gárab Dórjé had defeated him. The text that Mañjuṣrimitra then wrote exists to the present day.³

To understand in what sense the teaching of Gárab Dórjé can be said to be beyond the fundamental law of karma, the law of cause and effect, and thus apparently contradictory to the teaching of the Buddha, and yet nevertheless still be a perfect teaching, we must consider the famous 'Heart Sūtra', the essential summary of the vast Prajñāpāramitā sūtras. This sūtra proclaims the teaching on the nature of 'Śūnyatā', voidness, or emptiness, listing all the constituent elements with which we construct our reality, and stating that each in turn is void. Thus the sūtra expounds the voidness of the sense functions and their objects, repeating the formula: '. . . and so, because all phenomena are in essence void of self nature, the eye cannot be said to have any independent existence, and similarly there is in reality no such "thing" as an ear, or a nose . . . nor a faculty of seeing, nor of hearing, nor of smelling . . .', and so on. Then all the central elements of the Buddha's teaching are negated in the same way with a view to showing their essential voidness, and the sūtra states that from the point of view of emptiness '. . . there is no karma, no law of cause and effect'.

Since it is recorded in the sūtra that the great bodhissattva[4] Avalokitesvara was requested by the Buddha himself to give this teaching to another great bodhisattva, Mañjuṣri, in front of an assembled multitude of all kinds of beings, and since, at the end of the sutra, the Buddha greatly praises the wisdom of Avalokiteśvara's words, and it is recorded that the whole company rejoiced, it is clear that there is a teaching beyond cause and effect, and indeed beyond all limits, right at the heart of the Buddha's teachings themselves.

Gárab Dórjé had many disciples both among human beings and among the Ḍākinīs, and continued to teach for the rest of his life. Finally, before he dissolved his body into the essence of the elements and entered into the realization of the Body of Light, he left the summary of his teachings known as his 'Three Principles', which were presented above.

The Three Principles of Gárab Dórjé, the Three Series of the Zógqen teachings, and further Groups of Three

The Zógqen teachings, though their aim is not to develop the intellect, but to bring one beyond the intellect into the primordial state, contain a precise and crystalline structure of interlinked explanations. The Three Principles of Gárab Dórjé are the essentials of this crystalline structure, and all the various aspects of the teaching can be seen to be linked to them, in a network of interlocking components of explanation, grouped in threes. The diagram on p. 54 shows the correspondences between these groups of three.

The Three Principles of Gárab Dórjé begin with Direct Introduction, the direct transmission of the primordial state from the master to the disciple. It should be clear that this transmission itself is not something which comes within the realm of the intellect. But there are three ways in which the Introduction can be presented: direct, symbolic and oral. And these three styles of presentation are fundamental characteristics of what are known as the Three Series of Zógqen teachings: the Mannagdé or Essential Series; the Lóndé or Series of Space; and the Semdé or Series of the Nature of the Mind. A diagram of these Three Series is also included on p. 80, which shows the particular approach of each. The Three Series should not be seen as three grades, or divisions or a school. They are three modes of the presentation of Introduction, and three methods of practice, but they all aim to bring the practitioner to contemplation, and they are all equally Zógqen teachings. The division of Gárab Dórjé's teaching into Three Series was carried out by Mañjušrimitra, Gárab Dórjé's principal disciple, and continued by later masters.

The Mannagdé works most specifically on the principle of Direct Introduction (being the 'Essential Series'), the Lóndé adds a dimension of symbolic introduction, and the Semdé an oral introduction. So each Series has its particular way of presenting the introduction to contemplation and the primordial state, yet the same state is transmitted directly as an integral part of each Series. One can say that the Semdé is really the fundamental basis for the transmission of the Zógqen teachings, while the Lóndé works with the principle points of the Semdé; and the Mannagdé can be said to be the essential of the Semdé and the Lóndé, condensed by masters according to their experience and according to their discovery of 'derma' ('terma').[5] But the Semdé has tended to become rather

24

overshadowed by the presentation of the Mannagdé, and at various times it has been necessary to re-emphasize its importance.

CHAPTER 4

Zógqen in relation to the various levels of the Buddhist path

> Give up all negative actions;
> always act perfectly in virtue;
> develop complete mastery of
> your own mind:
> this is the teaching of the Buddha.
>
> Buddha Šākyamuni

> If thoughts arise,
> remain present in that state;
> if no thoughts arise,
> remain present in that state;
> there is no difference in the presence in either
>   state.
>
> Gárab Dórjé

The problem of dualism

It will be helpful in coming to an understanding of Zógqen to consider it in relation to the various other spiritual paths within the spectrum of Buddhism in general, which are all equally precious, and have been taught for the benefit of beings of different levels of capacity. These paths all have the common aim of seeking to overcome the problem that has arisen as the individual enters into dualism, developing a subjective self, or ego, that experiences a world-out-there as other, continually trying to manipulate that world in order to gain satisfaction and security. But one can never achieve satisfaction and security in this way, because all the seemingly external phenomena are impermanent and furthermore, the real cause of the suffering and dissatisfaction is the fundamental sense of incompleteness that is the inevitable consequence of being in the state of dualism.

Buddha Šākyamuni, the historical Buddha

The Buddha was a totally realized being who manifested a human birth in India, in the fifth century B.C., in order to be able to teach other human beings by means of his words and the example of his life. Suffering is something very concrete, which everyone knows and wants to avoid if possible, and the Buddha therefore began his teaching by talking about it in his famous first teaching called the 'Four Noble Truths'. The first truth draws our attention to the fact that we suffer, pointing out the existence of the basic dissatisfaction inherent in our condition; the second truth explains the cause of the dissatisfaction, which is the dualistic state of being we experience as a result of our grasping at phenomena and the desires that substantiate the existence of an ego as an entity separate from the integrated wholeness of the universe; the third truth teaches the possibility of the cessation of this suffering, through a return to the experience of integration in the overcoming of dualism; and the fourth truth explains the existence of a path to this cessation of suffering, which is the path that the Buddha taught.

SŪTRA:

All the various traditions are agreed that this basic problem of suffering exists, but they have different methods of dealing with it to bring the individual back to the experience of primordial unity. The Hinayāna tradition of Buddhism follows the Path of Renunciation that was taught by the Buddha in his human form and later written down in what are known as the 'Sūtras'. Here the ego is regarded as a poisonous tree, and the method applied is like digging up the roots of the tree one by one. One has to overcome all the habits and tendencies that are considered negative and hindrances to liberation. There are thus, at this level, many rules of conduct, governed by vows, that regulate all one's actions. The ideal is that of the monk or nun, who takes the maximum number of vows, but in any event, whether as a monk or a lay practitioner one's ordinary way of being is considered impure and to be renounced, in order, through the development of various states of meditation, to recreate oneself as a pure being who

Hinayāna
The Path of
Renunciation

has gone beyond the causes of suffering, an 'Arhat', who returns no more to the round of births and deaths in conditioned existence.

Mahāyāna

From the point of view of the Mahāyāna, to seek only one's own salvation in this way, and to go beyond suffering whilst others continue to suffer, is less than ideal. In the Mahāyāna it is considered that one should work for a greater good, putting the wish for the realization of all others before one's own realization, and indeed continually returning to the round of suffering to help others get beyond it. One who practises in this way is called a 'Bodhisattva'. Hinayāna, or 'Lesser Vehicle', and Mahāyāna, or 'Greater Vehicle', are both parts of the Path of Renunciation, but their characteristic approaches are different. To cut through the roots of a tree one by one takes a long time, and the Mahāyāna works more to cut the main root and then allow the other roots to wither by themselves by developing supreme compassion in the individual, as well as by working to realize the essential voidness of all phenomena and the ego, which is also the goal in the Hinayāna.

In the Mahāyāna, the intention behind one's actions is considered as important as one's actions themselves, which is a different approach from that of governing all one's actions with vows as one does in the Hinayāna. There is a story that illustrates this difference of approach very well. A wealthy merchant, who was a disciple of the Buddha, went with a very large caravan of other merchants and his servants to a certain island, to bring back for trade some of the gem stones for which this island was famous. On board ship, on the way back, the merchant learned that another passenger on the boat intended to kill all 300 people on board, in order to be able to steal the cargo of jewels. The merchant knew the man, and knew that he was indeed capable of killing all those people, and he wondered what to do about it. In the end, despite the fact that he had taken a vow with the Buddha never to take the life of another being, he had no alternative but to kill the would-be robber. He was very ashamed of what he had done, and as soon as he returned home he went to the Buddha to confess his bad action. But the Buddha told him he had not done wrong, because his intention had not been to take life, but to save life. Furthermore, since he had in fact saved the lives of 300 people, and had saved the robber from the very negative karma of killing 300 people and the inevitable consequences of such a bad action, the Buddha explained that the merchant had in fact done a good action. Because the intention behind one's actions is considered of such importance in the Mahāyāna, all practice is undertaken for the benefit of others.

Zen Buddhism is a Mahāyāna path, and because it is often said to be a 'non-gradual' method, people often think that it must be the same as Zógqen, which is also non-gradual; but their methods and the realizations obtained by them are fundamentally different.[1] Both the levels of the Path of Renunciation, Hinayāna and Mahāyāna can be said to work at the level of Body.

TANTRA:

Tantra, on the other hand, works at the level of Energy, or 'Voice'. Energy is obviously less concrete than body, and less easy to perceive. It is harder to understand energy and how it functions than to understand the simple fact of suffering. A higher capacity is therefore needed to practise tantra. Although the term 'tantra' has come to be used to denote a type of text that contains a tantric teaching, the true meaning of the word is 'continuation', in the sense that although all phenomena are void, nevertheless phenomena continue to manifest. All tantric methods work with this continuation, taking the voidness of all phenomena, which the sūtras work towards, as their basic assumption.

Vajrayāna
The Outer
tantras
The Path of
Purification

From the sūtra point of view, the relative dimension is an obstacle to be renounced in order to realize the absolute level of voidness. But tantra uses the relative to fuel progress on the path that leads beyond it, and its attitude to the passions renounced at the sūtra level is expressed in the tantric saying: 'When there is more wood (passions) there is more fire (realization).' There are Outer and Inner tantras, also called Lower and Higher tantras. Both these levels of tantra use visualization as a principle means, but the Outer tantras begin working at the level of the external conduct of the practitioner to bring about a purification of thought and action to prepare the practitioner to receive wisdom. The Outer tantras thus begin with what is called the Path of Purification, the first stage of the Vajrayāna, or 'Indestructible Vehicle'.

The Path of
Transformation

The second stage of the Vajrayāna is the Path of Transformation, which begins with the third and last level of the Outer tantras and includes all the three levels of the Inner tantras. These Inner tantras work once again on the basic assumption of the voidness of all phenomena, but they principally

The Inner
tantras

use inner yoga, working on the subtle energy system of the body, to bring about a transformation of the practitioner's whole dimension into the dimension of the realized being visualized in the practice. These methods were taught by the Buddha in a 'manifestation body', rather than by him in his physical body, as well as by other Sambhogakāya manifestations.

Transmission of tantra is originally received through a manifestation of the Sambhogakāya dimension appearing to a master who has sufficient visionary clarity to perceive that dimension, and the method of practice used in tantra is also that of manifestation. Once one is initiated into the practice by the master, through visualization and the reintegration of one's subtle energy, one follows the example of the original transmission, and manifests oneself as the deity, entering the pure dimension of the maṇḍala. Thus one realizes the Sambhogakāya oneself, transcending the mundane world of the gross elements, which are transformed into their essences. When one dies, one enters the dimension of light and colour that is the essence of the elements, and in that purified state of being, though not active in the individual sense, one remains capable of continually benefiting other beings. It is said that the developed tantric practitioner is like a baby eagle which is ready to fly as soon as it hatches from the egg: as soon as one dies, at that very moment, without entering the Bǎrdo, or intermediate state [see p. 162], one manifests as the divinity whose practice one has accomplished in one's lifetime. This realization is clearly different from the simple cessation of the round of birth and death which is aimed for in the Sūtra practices.

To develop sufficient mastery of the inner energy and sufficient power of concentration to complete this process of transformation, however, requires long years of solitary retreat, and is very difficult to achieve in one's daily life, even though it is a quicker method than the methods of the Path of Renunciation, which take many lifetimes to complete. But Zógqen is neither Sūtra nor Tantra. The basis for the communication of Zógqen is introduction, not manifestation as in tantra. Its *principal* practices work directly at the level of Mind to carry the individual into the primordial state, which is introduced directly by the master, in which state one continues until the total realization of the Great Transfer or the Body of Light are achieved. These are different again from the realizations arrived at through the practices of Sūtra and Tantra. I shall not discuss them here, however, but in the chapter on the Fruit of the Zógqen teachings [see pp. 116-35].

ZÓGQEN:
The Path of
Self-Liberation

Even though Zógqen is a teaching that works principally at the level of Mind, practices of the Voice and Body are found in the Zógqen teachings; but they are *secondary* to the practice of non-dual contemplation itself, and are used to bring the practitioner into this state. Only this contemplation can truly be called Zógqen, but a Zógqen practitioner may use practices from any of the levels of sūtra or tantra, if they are found to be necessary to remove obstacles that block the state of contemplation. The particular method of Zógqen is called the Path of Self-Liberation, and to apply it nothing need be renounced, purified, or transformed. Whatever arises as one's karmic vision is used as the path. The great master Pa Dǎmba Saṅgyás once said: 'It is not the circumstances which arise as one's karmic vision that condition a person into the dualistic state; it is a person's own attachment that enables what arises to condition him.' If this attachment is to be cut through in the most rapid and effective way, the mind's spontaneous capacity to self-liberate must be brought into play.

The term self-liberation should not, however, be taken as implying that there is some 'self' or ego there to be liberated. It is a fundamental assumption, as we have already said, at the Zógqen level, that all phenomena are void of self-nature. 'Self-Liberation', in the Zógqen sense, means that whatever manifests in the field of experience of the practitioner is allowed to arise just as it is, without judgment of it as good or bad, beautiful or ugly. And in that same moment, if there is no clinging, or attachment, without effort, or even volition, whatever it is that arises, whether as a thought or as a seemingly external event, automatically liberates itself, by itself, and of itself. Practising in this way the seeds of the poison tree of dualistic vision never even get a chance to sprout, much less to take root and grow.

So the practitioner lives his or her life in an ordinary way, without needing any rules other than his own awareness, but always remaining in the state of primordial unity by integrating his state with whatever arises as part of his experience, and with absolutely nothing to be seen outwardly to show that he is practising. This is what is meant by self-liberation, this is what is meant by the name Zógqen, which means 'Great Perfection', and this is what is meant by non-dual contemplation, or simply contemplation. Although in the course of my education in the monastic college in Tibet I came to study and practise all the various paths, my master Jyăñqub Dórjé helped me to understand the particular value of the Zógqen teachings, and so they are what I myself am principally concerned to teach.

The summary in chart form of the various paths of Sūtra, the levels of Tantra and Zógqen, that follows, has been included as an aid to getting clearly into view much of the terminology that is generally used in discussing the teachings. Despite the usefulness of such a chart, however, there is a danger that some readers may make the false assumption that it implies a hierarchy of teachings with Zógqen at the top. In fact, the whole layout could have been reversed, with Zógqen at the bottom; or the chart, as it now stands, could be read from the bottom up, which is the sequence in which the gradual paths are presented and practised, each stage having to be completed before the next can be approached. Zógqen differs from the gradual paths because the master introduces the disciple *directly* to the 'Great Perfection' which is the heart of all the paths. But the reason why so many paths exist is that there is thus a teaching suited to the capacity of every individual. So, for example, for someone to whom the sūtra teaching is best suited, that teaching can be said to be the 'highest', because that is the teaching that will work best for that individual. Any use of the words 'high', or 'highest', in relation to the Zógqen teachings, should be read with this important proviso in mind.

Summary of the methods of the various paths, of Sūtra, Tantra and Zógqen

Zógqen:	Not Sūtra, not Tantra, Zógqen does not see itself as the high point of any hierarchy of levels, and is not a gradual path. Zógqen is the Path of Self-Liberation, and not the Path of Transformation, so it does not use visualization as a principle practice; but it is beyond limits, and practices of any of the other levels can be used as secondary practices. The principal practice of Zógqen is to enter directly into non-dual contemplation, and to remain in it, continuing to deepen it until one reaches Total Realization.
Tantra:	The various levels of tantra are the practices of the *Vajrayāna*, and they work on the assumption of the voidness of all phenomena, the principle of Sūnyatā. They all work on this principle using visualization, but visualization is used differently at each level, with the aim of reintegrating the individual's energy with that of the universe.

Inner or Higher Tantras:	The Anuttara tantra (Supreme tantra; Tib: Sànva Lána Medbai Gyúddé) is divided into 3 levels in the Ñíñmaba school:—
(i) *Ati Yoga (Primordial Yoga)*:	Ati Yoga and Anu Yoga are only found in the Ñíñmaba (Nyingmapa) school. Ati Yoga is the final stage of the Anu Yoga, the culmination of the gradual path as seen in this school; Ati Yoga is also called Zógqen, and indeed the state reached in this Yoga is authentically the same as the state of Zógqen. But it is arrived at through the Path of Transformation, at the end of the nine stages of the gradual path, whereas Zógqen itself is non-gradual and in Zógqen Direct Introduction is given right away.
(ii) *Anu Yoga (Complete Yoga)*:	Leading to the Ati Yoga in the Ñíñmaba school, Anu Yoga uses a method of visualization only found in that school. The visualization is manifested in an instant, rather than built up gradually, detail by detail. One visualizes oneself as being the deity, and the sensation is more important than the details.
(iii) *Mahā Yoga (Great Yoga)*:	Whereas the culmination of the Path of Transformation in the Ñíñmaba school is the Ati Yoga, in the other three schools the practice of the Maha Yoga, involving gradual visualization detail by detail, leads to the state of the Mahāmudrā (Great Mudra, or Gesture). This state is once again not different to the state of Zógqen, or of Ati Yoga, though the method to arrive at it *is* different.

Outer or Lower Tantras: Yogatantra:	This is the first level of the Path of Transformation. Here one visualizes oneself as the 'deity' oneself, and begins the work with internal yoga using the subtle energy body, that continues in all the levels of the Path of Transformation above.
⸗ *Upāyatantra (Neutral or Intermediate tantra:*	The 'deity', or realized being is here visualized as external to oneself, though as one's equal, and one works with some inner yoga, as well as with external actions.
Kriyātantra (Action tantra):	This is the level of the Path of Purification and here one visualizes the deity as exterior to oneself, and superior to oneself. One works with external actions to purify oneself to be able to receive wisdom from the realized

35

being, and in preparation for working with the higher
levels of tantra.

Sūtra: *The Path*
of Renunciation:

Hinayāna and Mahāyāna work towards the experience of
Sūnyatā, or voidness, which is Tantra's basic assumption
and starting point. Gradual paths insist one must work
from here upwards. But Zógqen begins with the highest
teaching right away.

It was the great ninth-century A.D. master
Padmasambhava who was primarily responsible
for enabling the Buddhist teachings to become
established in Tibet, where obstacles had previously
been created by the shamanic practitioners of the
indigenous Bŏn traditions. Padmasambhava was a
totally realized being who manifested an extraordinary birth in Urgyán, where he received
visionary transmission of Zógqen directly from
Gárab Dórjé as well as oral transmission from lineal
descendents of Gárab Dórjé who were his con-
temporaries. Later he travelled to India, where he
absorbed and mastered all the tantric teachings
being taught there at that time. He developed the
capacity to transform himself into any form he
chose, as well as all the other 'siddhis', or powers
that may arise when the dualistic condition is
overthrown. Thus, when he was invited to go to
Tibet to further the spread of the Buddhist
teachings there, he was able to overcome the
obstacles that he encountered in the form of
negative energies, by means of his own superior
powers.

Every place has its governing energies, and the
Bŏn shaman priests had the capacity to focus the
various dominant energies of Tibet. They had used
this power to make it difficult for the Buddhist
teachings to take root there. Padmasambhava
manifested in various forms to gain mastery of the
local dominant energies himself, and to harness
them to protect the Buddhist teachings, of which
they then became the Guardians.

Since he was, however, beyond all limits, he did
not consider it necessary to reject what was of

Padmasambhava

Guru Drăgbo

Guru Drăgbo is a Heruka, and one of the principal
wrathful forms in which Padmasambhava manifested to
accomplish acts of power.

Siṃhamukha

The Ḍākinī Siṃhamukha is another of the
principal wrathful forms in which Padmasambhava
manifested.

value in the local traditions of Tibet, but instead created the conditions in which Buddhism could integrate with the local culture, with its sophisticated systems of cosmology, astrology, ritual and medicine, in the same way that Buddha Śākyamuni had taught within the framework of the Indian culture of his time, using it as the basis to communicate something essentially beyond culture. Thus, through Padmasambhava's influence and activity, there came into being that great confluence of spiritual traditions from Urgyán, India, and local Bŏnbo sources that is what we now know as the characteristically Tibetan form of Buddhism.

The original disciples of Padmasambhava in Tibet did not consider themselves a school, or sect. They were simply practitioners of tantric Buddhism and Zógqen.[2] But when there arrived later different traditions of practice following other lines of transmission from Indian tantric masters, and these developed as schools, the original followers of Padmasambhava became known as the 'Ñyíñmaba', the 'Ancient Ones', or 'Ancient School'.

One must be careful to avoid the mistake, however, of thinking that the Zógqen teachings are a school or sect, in themselves, or that they belong to any school or sect. What is meant by 'Zógqen' is always the primordial state. And although a lineage of transmission of this state from master to disciple does indeed exist, members of that lineage, all equally practitioners of Zógqen, could be and still can be found in all the schools of Tibetan Buddhism, or among the practitioners of Bŏn, or belonging to no school or sect at all.

A few examples may help to make this clear. My master Jyăñqub Dórjé was without limits and independent of schools. As well as receiving transmission from his principal master Ñgalà Padma Dúddùl, he received certain Zógqen teachings and transmissions from a Bŏnbo Zógqen master. In the Bŏn traditions there had existed a teaching of Zógqen right from the dawn of Tibetan history, though this tradition was not as fully developed as that introduced by Gárab Dórjé. The Nínmaba, or 'Ancient Ones', are the oldest of the four schools of

Tibetan Buddhism, and absorbed the Zógqen teachings at a very early date, still continuing to present them to the present day. So thoroughly has Zógqen become identified with the Ñíñmaba, however, that many have mistakenly assumed that Zógqen belongs only to that school. Very many great exponents of Zógqen have indeed manifested throughout the history of the Ñíñmaba, such as in relatively recent times, Lóñqen Rabjamba (1303–63) and Jìgmed Líñba (1729–98), who were among the greatest scholars, historians and spiritual teachers of Tibet. But another great Zógqen practitioner was the head of the Garma Gagyúd school. This was Rañjyúñ Dórjé (1284–1339), the third Garmaba (Karmapa), who integrated the Mahāmudrā teachings transmitted in the lineage of his school with the Ati Yoga tradition of Zógqen transmitted by the Ñíñmaba, and the transmission of the teachings thus integrated continues to the present day in the Gagyúd school.

The Sagyaba school evolved in the same period as the Gagyúd, following other lines of transmission received from the India Mahāsiddha tradition. My uncle Kyènze Qosgi Wáñqyug (Chentse Chosgi Wanchug) was an abbot of that school, and an outstanding example of the Zógqen practitioners among the Sagyaba. The most recently founded school, the Gelugba, evolved as a reform movement which saw itself as returning from what were regarded as the excesses of tantrism to a re-emphasis of the importance of the sūtra teachings, and to the strict application of the Vinaya, or rules of monastic conduct laid down by the Buddha. It is often therefore assumed that Zógqen must be very far from the Gelugpa ideal. Nevertheless, there have been many Zógqen masters in that school, including the great fifth Dalai Láma, Gyálqòg Nába (1617–82). He was the first Dalai Láma to hold the position of temporal ruler of Tibet as well as the spiritual role of his predecessors. It was he who began the building of the Potala Palace in its present form. He was a very great practitioner of Zógqen. So it should, in general, be remembered that masters with principal allegiance to the one

Tibetan wood-block print of the great fifth Dalai Láma, Gyálqòg Nába (1617–82), the first head of the Gelugpa school to be the temporal rule of Tibet. He was a great Zógqen practitioner.

Tibetan wood-block print of the third Garmaba, Rañjyŭn Dórjé (1284–1339), head of the Garma Gagyúd school, who integrated the Mahāmudrā and Ati Yoga traditions.

school, whilst fully maintaining that commitment, nevertheless freely received transmission from other traditions, and this in fact brought about a great cross fertilization in Tibetan spiritual life and culture.

CHAPTER 5

With my two uncles who were Zógqen masters

First cut through the confusion of learning.
Then ponder the meaning of what was learned;
And lastly meditate its meaning as instructed.

Milarasba

In Tibet masters could be found living in many different situations, but they had four principal types of life-style; those who were monks, living in monasteries; those who lived a lay life, with their homes in villages; lay masters who lived as tent-dwelling nomads, travelling with their disciples, in some cases following their herds;[1] and those who were yogis, often living in caves. I personally received transmission not only from my principal master, but also from many others, including my two uncles. My uncle Dogdán (Toden), was a great yogi, a practitioner of Zógqen. Like Jyǎñqub Dórjé, he did not have an intellectual education involving study, and was not attached to any school. In Dogdán's case this was because his parents had decided when he was very young that he should be a silversmith, and so his whole education was aimed at preparing him for his work as a craftsman. But at a certain point he became seriously mentally ill, and none of the doctors could cure him. Finally he was taken to see a Zógqen master of that time, Azòm Drùgba [see plate 1], and as a result of contact with this master he not only recovered from his illness but became a serious practitioner, a yogi who spent all his time in solitary retreats in isolated caves high in the mountains, where jaguars and leopards roamed. I was sometimes allowed to stay with him as a child,

45

and I remember that the leopards were particularly fond of butter, and that at night they would try to creep stealthily into the cave in which Dogdán stored his food to lick it up. I first learned Yantra Yoga in those high caves, as a very young boy, just copying Dogdán's movements. I first stayed with him when I was three years old, and I can remember my uncle practising Yantra for hours stark naked, while I amused myself as children of that age will, occasionally playfully slapping or kicking my uncle's bare back, as part of my games, while he continued his practice unperturbed. When I was a little older I learned the meaning of what he was doing.

Dogdán wore his hair long and had a big bushy beard, so that when I later came to the West I thought he bore a striking resemblance to the pictures I saw of Karl Marx, except that he didn't wear glasses. He was an example of the kind of practitioner who becomes recognized as a master through the qualities he or she manifests as a result of practice, rather than being recognized as the reincarnation of a previous master. When he was first sent to Azòm Drùgba he was so disturbed that he could hardly comprehend any of the teachings that were being given at his annual summer teaching retreat that was always held on the high plateau pasturelands in a village of tents, like a nomad encampment, that would arise for the duration of the retreat and then disappear again afterwards. By the time the retreat was over that summer, Dogdán had, with the help of Azòm Drùgba, been able to overcome his problem sufficiently to be ready to do some practice.

The master suggested that he make a solitary retreat, but because my uncle hadn't been able to follow the teachings he didn't know what to do in such a retreat. This is how Azòm Drùgba resolved the difficulty: he sent my uncle to a cave about four days journey away, telling him to stay there and practise until he sent for him, and he sent another disciple to show him the way to the cave. This other disciple had been following Azòm Drùgba for many years, and was a serious practitioner. He was

The practice of Jod

a simple man, not an intellectual, and he personally concentrated a great deal on the practice of the Jod (Chod). This is a practice in which one works to overcome attachment and ego-clinging by making a mentally visualized offering of one's own physical body. The practice was developed by a great Tibetan lady practitioner, Majig Labdrón[2] (1055–1149), who came from a Bönbo family and who combined elements from the Bönbo shamanic traditions with teachings of the Prajñapāramitā Sūtra and Zógqen traditions that she received from her two root masters, Pa Dǎmba and Drǎba Ñónxes, respectively, to produce a characteristically Tibetan form of practice which is a complete path in itself, but is also practised in conjunction with other methods. Practitioners of Jod are traditionally nomadic, travelling continually from place to place with a minimum of possessions, as mendicants, often carrying nothing more than the ritual instruments of a ḍamaru, or two sided drum, a bell, and a thigh bone trumpet, and living in a small tent set up using a ritual trident (kaṭvamga) as its tent pole, and four ritual daggers (purba) as its tent pegs. The practice is principally undertaken in lonely and desolate places, such as caves and mountain peaks, but in particular graveyards and charnel grounds at night, when the terrifying energy of such places serves to intensify the sensation of the practitioner who, seated alone in the dark, summons all those to whom he owes a karmic debt to come and receive payment in the form of the offering of his body. Among the invited are Buddhas and illuminated beings, for whom the practitioner mentally transforms the offering into nectar, and all the beings of the six realms, for whom the offering is multiplied and transformed into whatever will be of most benefit and most pleasing, but also summoned are demons and evil spirits to whom the body itself is offered as a feast just as it is. Internal 'demons' are all the usually latent fears, such as the fear of sickness or death, that can only be overcome when they are brought to the forefront of consciousness, but there also exist demons in the sense of negative energies that

Majig Labdrón (1055–1149) who first transmitted the Jod (Chod) as it is practised today. She is holding a bell and ḍamaru.

Tibetan wood-block print of a practitioner of the Jod,
practising in a charnel ground, sounding his ḍamaru and
thigh bone trumpet. His vajra and bell are on the ground
in front of him, together with an offering bowl made
from a human skull. The dancing, grinning skeletons at
the far right express a dynamic vision of death and
change, viewed as an ecstatic dance of transformation,
unchanging inner essence transcending the constant
mutations of externals. Meditation on the impermanence
of all phenomena should lead to a joyful freedom from
attachment, and not to a morbid pessimism.

the practice enables the practitioner to magnetize
and, ultimately, to master. We have an instinct for
self-protection, trying to defend ourselves from
imagined harm. But our attempt at self-protection
ultimately causes us more suffering, because it
binds us into the narrow dualistic vision of self and
other. By summoning up what is most dreaded,
and openly offering what we usually most want to
protect, the Jod works to cut us out of the double
bind of the ego and attachment to the body. In fact
the name 'Jod' means 'to cut'; but it is the
attachment, not the body itself that is the problem
to be cut through. The human body is regarded as
a precious vehicle for the attainment of realization.

The practitioner of Jod who accompanied my
uncle Dogdán to the cave in which he was to make
his solitary retreat led him by an extremely
circuitous route that travelled by way of so many

lonely spots favourable to his practice that instead of the usual four days, it took them well over a month to reach their destination. And on the way, each day, in the course of their ordinary conversation, he communicated straightforward instructions on all aspects of practice to my uncle, not just on the Jod, so that when he was finally left alone, Dogdán knew exactly what he should do.

My uncle stayed for several years in that retreat, and when he finally left it he had already developed the remarkable powers that led people to give him the name, or title, of 'Dogdán', which means 'Accomplished Yogi', by which I always refer to him, although his given name was Urgyán Danzìn. He continued thereafter to make frequent retreats, between which he travelled from place to place. His wanderings came to the attention of the Chinese authorities who were then making inroads into eastern Tibet, and they arrested him and called upon him to explain himself. Because of the way he was as an individual my uncle was not able to give them an answer to their satisfaction, and so they decided he must be a spy. His execution was ordered, but despite several attempts to shoot him, it proved impossible to kill him. When he was released, the people of the area began to call him 'Dogdán'. He could also communicate so well with animals that even the wild and timid mountain deer that normally ran away from everyone freely came to him and stayed wherever he did. Less docile creatures also frequented his company. On one occasion when the King of Dégé himself came to visit Dogdán, his minister climbed up to Dogdán's cave to announce the arrival of the King and found an enormous mountain lion seated peacefully beside the yogi. The King had no choice but to share the company of that most royal of beasts if he wished to be received. This he did, with no little trepidation.

Living as he did, far from any centres of habitation, considerable hardship was involved for all those who gradually heard of Dogdán's reputation as a practitioner and came to seek him out to receive teachings from him. The same was also true of my other uncle, Kyènze Qosgi Wáñqyug, although the circumstances of his early life had been very different from Dogdán's. He had been recognized at an early age as a drulgu, and was enthroned as the reincarnation of the Abbot of four important monasteries. In this position he was expected to conform to a certain pattern of life involving administrative and even political duties, as well as fulfilling scholarly and ritual obligations. He, however, despite considerable opposition, preferred to spend his time in retreat, dedicating his life to practice.

When in retreat he, too, lived in remote isolation, in his case in a cave above the snow line, where there was snow all the year round. But such was his reputation as a practitioner, and in particular as a derdon or discoverer of hidden texts and objects, that he was sought out by those determined to receive teachings from him. Strange things frequently happened around Kyènze Qosgi Wáñqyug connected with his capacity as a derdon. On one occasion, when I was still quite young, I went to stay in a cave close to, but a little below my uncle's. While there, I had a dream one night, in which a Ḍākinī appeared to me and gave me a small scroll of paper on which there was written a sacred text. She explained that the text was very important, and that on waking I should give it to my uncle. By this time my practice had already developed to the extent that I could maintain awareness throughout my sleep and dreams, and in this dream I knew that I was dreaming. I remember closing one of my fists around the scroll, and then closing the other fist tightly around the first.

The rest of the night passed uneventfully, and when I awoke at dawn, I found that my fists were still tightly clenched one around the other. When I opened my hands, I found that there really was a small scroll in the palm of one hand. I at once went in great excitement to knock on the door of my uncle's cave. It was not normally permitted to disturb him at such an early hour, as he would be engaged in his morning session of practice, but I was too excited to wait. He came to the door, and I explained what had happened and showed him the scroll. He looked at it for a moment, quite calmly, and said: 'Thank you. I was expecting this.' Then he went back to his practice as if nothing extraordinary had happened at all.

On another occasion he asked my advice about a vision he had had of where a derma would be discovered. He always very kindly showed great respect for my opinions, although I was still quite young. He was not sure whether to make a public announcement about the derma, or whether to go about finding it quietly. I felt it could be of benefit to many beings, in confirming and developing their faith, if many people knew about it and were present when it was found. My uncle agreed to this, and the announcement was made, declaring that the derma was located in a certain area, and that we would go to find it on a certain date.

When the appointed day came, we went out, and were soon accompanied by a large crowd of people. The place my uncle had indicated was high up on the side of a mountain, and as he was an enormously fat man, he had to be carried by four men to get up there. Finally he said that we had arrived close enough and pointed to a smooth, sloping rock face some way above us. He said that the derma was within the rock there. He then asked for a small ice-pick, of the sort that climbers use and when one was given to him, he stood with it in his hand in silence for a few minutes, before throwing it with all his might up towards the rock face. The pick lodged firmly in what looked like solid rock, and held there. My uncle said that that was where the derma would be, and as everyone else watched, several of the younger men present made a ladder from a tree trunk, and set it in position to climb up. One young man then climbed carefully up and removed the pick. To everyone's amazement a certain amount of rock came away from what had looked like solid stone. My uncle then told the young man to search gently with the pick in the opening thus revealed. It was full of loose dry sand. My uncle told him to pull it out, and he very slowly did so. Then he stopped and gasped, perched high above us on the ladder. He said that he could see a smooth, round, luminous white object. My uncle told him not to touch it. A blanket was then spread out below, held fairly taut between several people, and, using the pick, the young man up the ladder caused the object to fall into the blanket. My uncle then picked it up in a white silk scarf, and when he held it up we all saw the mysterious luminous white orb, made of no material known to us, and about the size of a large grapefruit.

When we returned home my uncle closed the object in a special wooden container that was locked, and secured with a wax seal. He said that it would reveal itself further later. But when after several months we opened the still sealed container, the object had mysteriously vanished. My uncle did not seem surprised, but said that the Ḍākinīs had taken it back, as the time was not yet ripe for its discovery and revelation.

As I have already said, strange things frequently happened around my uncle, and partly as a result of them many people sought teachings from him. It was a long climb to get to his cave from the forest far below, but nevertheless sometimes twenty or thirty people would make the tremendous effort to climb up to see him. Then his cave was very small, and all twenty or thirty people would have to squeeze inside, and sit really squashed together to hear him teach. Kyènze Qosgi Wáñqug didn't plan to make it hard for people, it's just that these were the conditions he himself lived in. Then, at the end of the day, all those who had come for teachings would have to climb down the steep mountain-side in the dark – and we didn't have flashlights in Tibet! When they got to the bottom, they would spend the night in the forest, sleeping rough; there was no hotel there. And the next morning they would climb all the way up again to receive more teachings.

But even this hardship was nothing compared to the effort Milarasba (Milarepa) had to make to receive teachings from his master Marbá,[3] who made him build five towers and pull each one down again before he would give him any teaching. To understand why these people were prepared to endure all this hardship, we need to remember how fragile our lives are, and that death can come for any of us at any time. Knowing how we continue to suffer in life after life without understanding why we are suffering or how we can bring this suffering to an end, the enormous value of a master and his or her teaching becomes urgently clear.

It is not unusual for people to make great efforts and sacrifices to receive the teachings. But there is a tendency to want things made easy that is particularly common today. Here in this book it may seem that the explanations that follow of the Base, the Path and the Fruit, as they are understood in the Zógqen teachings are complex, and that much effort is needed to understand them. Yet the effort required cannot be compared to the effort needed if one were to seek an explanation from a master such as Dogdán, Kyènze Qosgi Wáñqyug, or Marbá. No matter how clear a given explanation may be, without the active participation of the one who is to receive nothing can be communicated. If an attempt is to be made sincerely to explain the nature of the universe and the nature of the individual, it cannot be expected that it will be as easy to read as a good story; and yet it need not be so very complicated either!

There is a classic pattern of explanation of the teaching using a framework of interrelated concepts grouped in threes, and it is this pattern that the explanation given below will follow. The bones of this pattern can be shown simply in the form of a diagram:

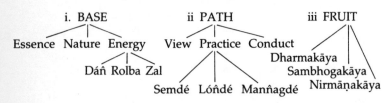

(a more complex version of this diagram will be found on p. 136)

54

The Base, the Path, and the Fruit

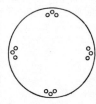

The Zógqen teachings are also known in Tibetan by another name, 'Tigle Qenbo', or 'Great Tigle', and a *tigle* is a spherical drop-like form, with no dividing lines or angles, like the representation, left above, of the circular mirror, or *meloñ*, made of five precious metals that is a particular symbol of the Zógqen teachings and of the unity of the primordial state. So, although the teachings are divided into groups for the purpose of clear explanation, their fundamental unity, like the perfect sphere of the *tigle*, must not be forgotten. But within this fundamental unity the groups of three are distinguished, each one interconnected with all the others, as represented in the design,

shown left, with its triangular divisions, concentric circles, and the 'Gákyìl', or 'Wheel of Joy', whirling at the centre. Around the edge of this design (lower left), from the obverse of a contemporary meloñ, the syllables Hă A Ha Sha Sa Ma which close the gates to the six realms are written in an ancient script of Xăñxuñ.

CHAPTER 6

The Base

It is quite impossible to find the Buddha
anywhere other than in one's own mind.
A person who is ignorant of this
may seek externally,
but how is it possible to find oneself
through seeking anywhere other than in oneself?
Someone who seeks their own nature externally
is like a fool who,
giving a performance in the middle of a crowd,
forgets who he is
and then seeks everywhere else to find himself.

Padmasambhava (The Yoga of Knowing the Mind)

Of the groups of three, the group known as 'The Base, the Path, and the Fruit'[1] is of central importance, and we shall now consider each of these in turn.

The Base: $\begin{cases} \text{essence} \\ \text{nature} \\ \text{energy} \end{cases}$

The Base, or 'Xi', in Tibetan, is the term used to denote the fundamental ground of existence, both at the universal level, and at the level of the individual, the two being essentially the same; to realize the one is to realize the other. If you realize yourself you realize the nature of the universe. We have previously referred to the primordial state, experienced in non-dual contemplation, and it is in this state that the individual regains the experience of identity with the Base. It is called the Base because it is there from the very beginning, pure and self-perfected and does not have to be constructed. It exists in every being, and cannot be destroyed, though the experience of it is lost when a being enters into dualism. It is then temporarily obscured by the interaction of the negative mental states of the passions of attachment and aversion that arise from the root ignorance of dualistic vision. But the Base should not be objectified as a self-existent thing, it is a state, or condition of being. In an ordinary individual it is latent; in a realized individual it is manifest.

In the teachings in general, not just in the Zógqen teaching, it is considered that consciousness does not cease with the death of the physical body, but transmigrates, the karmic causes accumulated over countless lifetimes giving rise to further rebirths until the individual becomes realized, karma is transcended, and transmigration is brought to an end. The question of how and when this transmigration began is not so much spoken of, because it is considered more important to deal with those things that will actually be helpful in bringing the suffering of transmigration in conditioned existence to an end, rather than to waste one's precious time speculating about a first cause. At the time of the Buddha there was considerable debate amongst the Brahmin sects as to the precise nature of the Creator, and even as to whether a Creator existed. But the Buddha himself refused to either confirm or deny the existence of a Supreme Being as first cause, advising his disciples to apply themselves to reaching the state of enlightenment, in which state they would know for themselves the answers to such questions beyond doubt or speculation.

At the level of what we ourselves actually experience in our lives it is clear where transmigration begins: it begins in any instant in which we enter into dualism, just as it ends when we enter the primordial state, which is beyond all limits, including the limits of time, and of words and concepts. Nevertheless the words of the Song of Vajra[2] try to describe it:

The Song of the Vajra

Unborn,
yet continuing without interruption,
neither coming nor going,
                              omnipresent,

Supreme Dharma,
unchangeable space, without definition,
spontaneously self-liberating

– perfectly unobstructed state –
existing from the very beginning,
self-created, without location,
with nothing negative to reject,
and nothing positive to accept,
infinite expansion, penetrating everywhere,
immense, and without limits, without ties,
with nothing even to dissolve,
or to be liberated from

present beyond space and time,
existing from the beginning,
immense 'yíñ',* inner space,
radiant through clarity like the sun and the moon,
self-perfected,

indestructible like a Vajra,
stable as a mountain,
pure as a lotus,
strong as a lion,
incomparable pleasure
beyond all limits,
illumination,
equanimity,
peak of the Dharma,
light of the universe,
perfect from the beginning.

* Tibetan Yíñ; Sanskrit Dhatu dimension.

The Self-
Origination of the
five elements and
their essences

Just as the conditioned existence of the individual arises from karmic traces, so too does the existence of whole universes. The ancient Tibetan Bön tradition of cosmology, for example, explains that the space that existed before the creation of this universe was the latent karmic trace remaining from beings of previous universal cycles that had since gone into destruction. This space moved within itself, and the essence of the element wind was formed; the ferocious friction of this wind against itself gave rise to the essence of the element fire; resulting differences in temperature caused the condensation of the essence of the element water; and the swirling of these three already existing essences of elements gave rise to the essence of the element earth, in the same way that churning milk causes it to solidify into butter. This level of the essence of the elements is a pre-atomic level of existence as light and colour. From the interaction of all the essences of the elements, the actual elements at an atomic, or material, level are formed, in the same manner and sequence that the essences of the elements were formed. Then from the interaction of the material, or atomic, elements, what is called the 'Cosmic Egg', made up of all the various realms of being, is formed. These realms are those of the higher Divinities and Nāgas, as well as the six realms of conditioned existence: those of the Gods and Demi-Gods, Humans and Animals, the Frustrated Spirits and the Hell Beings.

If the essences of all the elements, and thus the elements themselves[3] and all the various realms arise from space, which is the latent karmic traces of past beings, this space is not beyond karma, thus not beyond the conditioned level of existence. It cannot be said to be fundamentally pure from the beginning and self-perfected, which is the condition of the Base. Thus the primordial state, 'Unborn, yet continuing without interruption, neither coming, nor going, omnipresent . . . beyond space and time . . . existing from the beginning . . .', in the words of the Song of the Vajra, could be said to be like the essence of the element space, omnipresent and unborn, yet the ground of all being.

The Zógqen teachings themselves view the process of cosmic origination in a way that is parallel to, but slightly different from, the Bŏn tradition. In the Zógqen teachings, it is considered that the primordial state, which is beyond time, and beyond creation and destruction, is the fundamentally pure base of all existence, both at the universal and the individual levels. It is the inherent nature of the primordial state to manifest as light, which in turn manifests as the five colours, the essences of the elements. The essences of the elements interact (as explained in the Bŏn cosmology) to produce the elements themselves, which make up both the individual's body, and the whole material dimension. The universe is thus understood as the spontaneously arising play of the energy of the primordial state, and may be enjoyed as such by an individual who remains integrated with his or her essential inherent condition, in the self-liberating, self-perfected state, the state of Zógqen. But if, through fundamental misperception of reality, the individual enters into the confusion of dualism, primordial consciousness, which is in fact the source of all manifestation, becomes caught up in its own projections, which it then takes as an external reality existing separately from itself. All the various passions arise from this fundamental misperception, and continually condition the individual into dualism.

The Zógqen teachings, in the explanations of the Base, the Path, and the Fruit, set out to show how the illusion of dualism has come about, how it can be undone, and what the experience of an individual is when it is undone. But all examples used to explain the nature of reality can only ever be partially successful in describing it, because it is, in itself, beyond words and concepts. As Milarasba said, we may say that the essential nature of the mind is like space, because both are empty, but mind is aware, while space is not. Realization is not knowledge *about* the universe, but the living experience of the nature of the universe. Until we have such living experience, we remain dependent on examples, and subject to their limits. We could say that the Base is like a mysterious object that I am trying to describe to you. I might say that the object is white and sort of round, and then you'll get a certain idea of it; but the next day you might hear another description given by someone else who has seen it, and then you'll change your mind according to their description, thinking perhaps that the object is rather more oval than round, and the colour of mother of pearl rather than white. Fifty descriptions later, you're not really any the wiser about the object, still changing your mind each time you hear it described. But if you once see the object for yourself, then you know for sure what it's like, and you understand that all the descriptions were right, in part, but none really could catch the whole nature of that mysterious object. That's how it is with any description of the Base, the primordial state that remains the true inherent condition of the individual, pure from the beginning, even if a being is immersed in dualism and enmeshed in the passions.

Now that we have considered the meaning of the term 'Base' as it is understood in the Zógqen teachings, we can begin to consider how this Base manifests as the individual and the universe he or she experiences. All levels of the teachings regard the individual as being made up of Body, Voice, and Mind. The perfected states of these are symbolized by the Tibetan syllables Om, â, and Hûm, respectively. Body includes the whole material dimension of the individual, while Voice is the vital energy of the body, known as prāṇa in Sanskrit, and lùn̄ in Tibetan, the circulation of which is linked to the breathing. Mind includes both the mind that reasons, and the nature of the mind, which is beyond the intellect. The body, voice and mind of an ordinary being have become so conditioned that he or she has become completely caught up in dualism. Such a being's dualistic perception of reality is called impure or karmic vision, as it is conditioned by the karmic causes continually manifesting as a result of one's past

Om

â

Hûm

The Wheel of Existence

Pure and
impure vision

actions, to the extent that one lives enclosed in the world of one's limits, like a bird in a cage. But a realized being, who is beyond the limits of dualism, who has made real or realized the previously only latent condition of the Base, is said to have pure vision.

With the perfected clarity of this primordial state of pure vision, realized beings have accompanied their direct transmission of the state they dwell in with an oral explanation of the Base. This explanation shows how the ground of existence experienced by the individual functions as what are called the Three Wisdoms or Three Conditions, Essence, Nature, and Energy, and to illustrate their functioning a mirror, a crystal, and a crystal ball are used.

Tibetan wood-block print showing Yama, the god of death, holding the 'Wheel of Existence'. At the centre, the cock, snake and pig symbolize the 'Three Poisons': dualistic mind (or ignorance; pig), which gives rise to aversion (snake), and attachment (cock), which lock an individual into a vicious cycle of self-sustaining suffering (Sanskrit: Saṃśara). In the next circle, preceding outwards from the centre, beings are shown either progressing upwards towards realization through spiritual practice, or falling downward becoming more caught up in transmigration in the six realms of conditioned existence, which are shown in the next, and widest circle. The three higher realms are shown in this version of the Wheel in two segments of the circle to the left and right of the 12 o'clock position. The gods' and demi-gods' realms are shown as one on the left, and the human realm is shown on the right. Continuing clockwise, there are the realm of the pretas or continually frustrated spirits, the realm of hell beings, and the realm of the animals. The human realm is the most favourable for progress to realization. The outer circle symbolizes the twelve links of the 'Chain of Interdependent Origination', which explains how in every instant dualistic experience is solidified out of the open space of primal awareness through fundamental misperception of reality and the ensuing mental processes, thus creating the illusion of conditioned existence in the six realms.

Essence   The aspect of the Base that is referred to as the 'Essence' is its fundamental voidness. Practically speaking, this means that, for example, if one looks into one's own mind, any thought that arises can be seen to be void in the three times, past, present, and future. That is to say, if one looks for a place from which the thought came, one finds nothing; if one looks for a place where the thought stays, one finds nothing; and if one looks for a place where the thought goes, one finds nothing: voidness. It is not that there is some 'void' that could be said to be some sort of 'thing', or 'place' itself, but rather that all phenomena, whether mental events, or apparently 'external' actual objects, no matter how solid they may seem, are in fact essentially void, impermanent, only temporarily existing, and all 'things' can be seen to be made up of other things, in turn made up of other things, and so on. From the enormously large, to the infinitely small, and everywhere in between, everything that can be seen to exist can be seen to be void. And by way of an example, this voidness is said to be like the fundamental purity and clarity of a mirror. A master may show the disciple a mirror and explain how the mirror itself does not judge the reflections arising in it to be either beautiful or ugly: the mirror is not changed by whatever kind of reflection may arise, nor is its capacity to reflect impaired. It is then explained that the void nature of the mind is like the nature of the mirror, pure, clear and limpid, and that no matter what arises, the void essence of the mind can never be lost, damaged or tarnished.

Nature   Yet, even if voidness is the essential underlying condition of all phenomena, phenomena – whether as mental events or as actual experienced objects – still continue to manifest. Things continue to exist, thoughts continue to arise, just as reflections continue to arise in a mirror, even though they are void. And this continual arising is what is meant by the aspect of the Base that is called its 'Nature'. Its Nature is to manifest, and by way of example, this Nature is compared to the inherent capacity of the mirror to reflect whatever is put in front of it.

The master may again use an actual mirror to show that whether what is reflected be good or bad, beautiful or ugly, the mirror's inherent capacity to reflect functions just the same as soon as an object is placed before it. It is then explained that the same is true of what is referred to as the nature of the mind, which is experienced in contemplation. Any thought or event may arise, but the nature of the mind will not be conditioned by it. The nature of the mind does not enter into judgment, it simply reflects in the same way that the nature of a mirror does.

Energy

So the Xí, the Base, the fundamental condition of the individual and of existence, is in Essence void, and yet its Nature is nevertheless to manifest. How it manifests is as Energy, and by way of example this Energy is compared to the reflections that arise in a mirror. The master may once again show a mirror to the disciple and explain how the reflections that arise in it are the energy of the mirror's own inherent nature manifesting visibly. But the example of the mirror shows that the Essence, Nature, and Energy are all mutually interdependent, and cannot truly be separated from each other, except for the purposes of explanation. This is because the purity and clarity of a mirror, its capacity to reflect, and the reflections that arise in it, are all essential for what we know as a mirror to exist. If there is no clarity, the mirror will not reflect; if there is not capacity to reflect, how can there be reflections? And if there is no possibility of the arising of reflections, how can there be a mirror? This is also how it is with the three aspects of the Base: Essence, Nature, and Energy. They are interdependent.

**How the Energy manifests:
Zal, Rolba, Dáñ**

Now this Energy has three characteristic ways of manifesting, which are known as Dáñ, Rolba and Zal (Tsal). These terms are untranslatable, and we have to use the Tibetan words. They are explained by three examples.

Zal

Zal refers to the way in which it is the very Energy of the individual him or herself that appears as a seemingly external world. A being who has entered into dualism thus experiences living in a closed off self, seemingly separate from a world 'out there', which is experienced as other, and mistakes the projections of his own senses for objects existing as separate from this self he clings on to. The example used to show the illusion of this separateness draws a parallel between the way the individual's energy manifests, and what happens when a crystal is placed in the sunlight. In the same way that the sun's light, falling on the crystal, is reflected and refracted by it, causing the appearance of rays and patterns of spectral colours that seem to be separate from the crystal yet in fact are functions of its own characteristic nature, so, too, it is the individual's own energy perceived by that individual's own senses that appears as a world of apparently external phenomena. In truth, there is nothing external or separate from the individual, and the fundamental unity of 'what is', is precisely what is experienced in Zógqen, the Great Perfection. For a realized being, this level of one's own energy manifesting as Zal is the dimension of the Nirmāṇakāya – or 'Manifestation Body'. So when we speak of the 'Three Kayas', or bodies, these do not just mean three bodies of the Buddha, or three levels of a statue. They are three dimensions of the energy of every individual, as experienced in realization [see p. 129].

Rolba

A crystal ball is used as the example for this way in which the energy of the individual manifests. When an object is placed near a crystal ball, an image of that object may be seen inside the crystal ball, so that the object itself seems to be within. Thus the Energy of the individual may appear as an *'internally'* experienced image, seen as if 'in the mind's eye'. Yet, no matter how vivid this image may be, it is nevertheless once again the individual's own Energy manifesting, this time as *Rolba*. It is at this level that the practitioner of the Path of

Transformation works to transform impure vision into pure vision, by the power of concentration. And for a realized being, this level of his or her own energy is experienced as the Sambhogakāya, or 'Body or Wealth'. The wealth referred to here is the fantastic multiplicity of forms that can manifest at this level, the level of the essence of the elements, which is light. For example, the one hundred peaceful and wrathful divinities described in the Bărdo Tosdrŏl, or Tibetan Book of the Dead, as arising to the consciousness in the Bărdo, are manifestations of this level of the individual's own Energy.[4]

Dáń

A crystal ball has no colour. But when it is placed on a red cloth, it seems to be red; then again, on a green cloth, it seems to be green, and so on. In just the same way, at the level of *Dáń*, the Energy of the individual is essentially infinite and formless; yet it can take any form whatsoever. This example helps to clarify what is meant by karmic vision: although the individual's energy is essentially without form, as a result of attachment, the karmic traces that exist in the stream of consciousness of the individual give rise to what is perceived as a body, voice, and mind, and as external environment, whose characteristics are determined by the causes accumulated over countless lives. In the illusion of duality, the individual is so conditioned by this karmic vision, that it in fact seems to be what the individual is.

When this illusion is cut through the individual experiences his or her own condition as it truly is, and was from the beginning: infinite mind, energy beyond all limits of form whatever. To realize this is to realize the 'Dharmakāya', or 'Body of Truth', better rendered as the 'Body of Reality as it is'. But neither *Dáń*, *Rolba*, and *Zal*, nor Dharmakāya, Sambhogakāya, and Nirmāṇakāya, are separate from each other. Infinite, formless energy (Dharmakāya) manifests at the level of the essence of the elements, which is light, as non material forms only perceivable by those with visionary clarity (Sambhogakāya), and at the level of matter in apparently solid material forms (Nirmāṇakāya).

So, by means of these examples, an oral introduction is given by the master to the Base, and an explanation is made of the way in which it manifests as the three modes of energy. This is the open secret, which all can discover for themselves. We live our lives, as it were, 'inside out', projecting the existence of an 'I' as separate from an external world which we try to manipulate to gain satisfaction. But as long as one remains in the dualistic state, one's experience has always underlying it a sense of loss, of fear, of anxiety, and dissatisfaction.

When, on the other hand, one goes beyond the dualistic level, anything is possible. Near the cave of Milarasba there lived a very scholarly Tibetan monk who saw himself as being very intelligent. He believed he could overcome everything with his intellect, but the strange thing was that everyone went to receive teachings from Milarasba who had never studied anything, and no one came to see this monk. The monk was very jealous, and went to see Milarasba to debate with him. He wanted to expose him with a few well chosen words of argument, so he asked: 'Is space material or immaterial?' Milarasba replied: 'It's material!' The monk thought to himself: 'Now I've shown him up as a complete idiot!', and was preparing to debate some more in the same way, when Milarasba picked up a stick and began banging on empty space as if it were a drum. The monk then asked: 'Is a rock material or immaterial?' Milarasba replied by passing his hand through a rock. The amazed monk became his disciple.

The intellect is a valuable tool, but it doesn't extend to the fullness of our being. In fact it can be a trap preventing our gaining access to the most profound aspects of our own nature. When I was young, I met a very strange master whose activities were as unfathomable to the intellect as Milarasba's, though his life story was very different. He had formerly been a monk in a Sagyaba monastery, which like all monasteries had certain very strict rules. This monk had broken the rules in a very serious way by having a relationship with a woman, and he had been expelled from the monastery. He felt bad about what had happened, and so he went very far away, but on his travels he met some masters, received some teachings from them, and became a serious practitioner. Then he returned to his native village, but the monastery there wouldn't take him back in, so his relatives built him a little retreat hut on the mountainside. He lived there practising quietly for several years, and became known to everyone as 'The Practitioner'.

But after a few more quiet years he suddenly seemed to go crazy. One day while he was doing his practice he began to throw all of his books out of the window; then he burned them, smashed up all his statutes, turned everything upside down, and partly destroyed his retreat house. People began to call him 'The Lunatic'. Then he disappeared, and no one saw him for three years. At the end of that time somebody came across him quite by chance. He was living in a very remote spot, right at the top of the mountain. Everybody wondered how he had managed to survive and get enough to eat up there all that time, because nothing grew there and nobody normally ever went there. So people began to take an interest in him and to visit him. Although he refused to communicate with them, the way that he lived convinced people that he wasn't crazy. Instead of calling him 'The Lunatic', they began to speak of him as a realized being, a saint.

My uncle the Sagyaba abbot, Kyènze Qosgi Wáñqyug, heard about him, and decided to visit him, taking me and a few other people with him. It took us fifteen days on horseback to get to the village below the mountain where the strange master lived. From there we would have to climb up on foot, as there was no track to the mountain top, which was very difficult to get up to. The people of the area told us that some days previously a very famous Gagyud drulgu incarnation had gone up there to visit, but when he arrived, instead of receiving teaching, he'd been driven off with a barrage of stones, and some of the monks in his party had been quite badly hurt.

They also told us that this master up there had dogs, and that some of them were fierce and would bite. All of the local people were afraid of going to see him, and by the time we'd heard all this, quite frankly, so were we.

My uncle was a very fat man, and to climb the steep mountainside without a path took us a very long time. We were always slipping and sliding back down on the loose rock. When we had almost reached the top we could hear the master talking somewhere, but we couldn't see a house anywhere. Then when we finally arrived at the very peak of the mountain we saw a kind of rudimentary stone structure. You couldn't really call it a house, it was more like a big dog kennel roofed over with stones, with big open holes in three of its sides. It wasn't high enough for anyone to be able to stand up in. We could hear the master still talking inside, but we couldn't imagine who he might be talking to.

Then he turned and saw us approaching, so he at once pretended to be asleep, pulling a blanket up over his head. He really did seem crazy, but we cautiously went even closer. When we got quite close we waited a few minutes and then he suddenly pulled the blanket away from his face and looked at us. His enormous staring eyes were bloodshot, and his hair stood wildly on end. I found him really terrifying. He began to speak, but we couldn't understand what he was saying, even though he was a Tibetan like us. It was not that he was speaking in a local dialect that we didn't understand; we knew the dialect of that area quite well. He spoke for about five minutes without interruption, but I only understood two phrases. Once he seemed to be saying 'in the middle of the mountains', but then what he said next was incomprehensible again. The next phrase I caught seemed to be 'worth it' and then nothing meant anything again. I asked my uncle what he had understood, but he had only caught the same two fragments, and none of the other people with us had understood any more either.

My uncle crawled in through the largest of the openings in the stone wall, perhaps with the intention of asking for a blessing to see what the reaction would be. The hut was very small and he was very big, and the strange master stared right into his face. My uncle had brought some sweets with him, and he offered two of these to the master, who took just one. The master had a kind of earthenware pot by his side. He put the sweet in the pot and offered it back to my uncle. My uncle just stayed in there waiting. Then the master pulled out from a fold in his tattered clothes a piece of old woollen cloth which he had clearly used for blowing his nose, and he presented this to my uncle. My uncle accepted it respectfully and continued waiting, until the master gave him a very fierce look, at which my uncle decided it was wisest to come out.

It was then my turn to go in. I was very frightened, but in I went, with a packet of biscuits which my uncle had given me to offer. I offered the packet, but the master wouldn't take it. I thought: 'Maybe I should have opened the packet first', so I opened it and offered him some biscuits. He took one and put it in his pot. I managed to get a look into the pot, and saw that it was full of water, but that it also contained a bit of everything, some tobacco, some peppers, and my uncle's sweet, together with my biscuit. I don't know if he ate from this pot or if he just kept things in it, but there was nothing in that hut that suggested the normal domestic activities of preparing and cooking food, even if its inhabitant could have found some up there. I stayed a little longer taking all this in, until with a ferocious look the master gave me a sort of half broken earthenware teapot which he used as a piss-pot, and then, taking this gift with me, I left to rejoin my uncle and the others outside.

We'd been there about twenty minutes in all, and we stood outside looking in at him. Then he began speaking to us again incomprehensibly and pointing, and we got the idea that he was trying to tell us to go in that direction. We waited there a little longer, when he suddenly said, rather angrily and quite coherently: 'Better to go!' My uncle turned to me and the rest of our little group and said: 'Maybe we had better do as he says!', and we all set off in the direction the strange master had pointed to. It wasn't the way we had come and would have to go back, and we hadn't the faintest idea where we were going or why, but my uncle said that there might be something behind what the master had said. It was very rough going but we clambered along and down from that peak for several hours, to the place where the mountain began to rise again towards the next peak. In what you might call the saddle between the two peaks there was a heavily forested area, and just before we got down to that we heard what sounded like someone groaning and crying out. We hurried forward and found a hunter who had fallen from the rocks and broken his foot. He was unable to walk, and so some of our group carried him back to where his family lived, which was some considerable distance away. My uncle suggested that the rest of us go back to see the strange master. 'Perhaps he'll give us some teaching now', he said. But when we got back to the strange master's hut, far from saying anything like 'Well done!', he just told us to go away.

But the fact that a master like this was not commited to teaching human beings doesn't necessarily mean that he wasn't teaching at all. He might have been living in that strange way while manifesting in another dimension to teach beings other than humans. In that way he could have been giving teaching to more beings than there are in a whole huge city, while we did not have the capacity to perceive such activity. Gárab Dórjé, for example, taught the Zógqen teachings to the Dākinīs before teaching them to human beings. In the Bărdo, the intermediate state after the death of the physical body and preceding the next rebirth of the aggregates of the consciousness of the deceased, beings exist in a mental body with no physical connection or counterpart. It is possible that this master who seemed so strange to us was teaching such beings. When we understand the non-dual nature of reality as described in the explanations of the Base as Essence, Nature and Energy, and know how the Energy of the individual manifests as Dáñ, Rolba and Zal, we can understand how someone who has reintegrated their Energy is capable of actions not possible for an ordinary being. Then the actions of such a master no longer seem so incomprehensible.

CHAPTER 7

The Path

Some people spend the whole of their life
preparing to practise; then the end of
their life comes, and they are still preparing.
So they begin their next life without ever
having completed all these preparations!

Drăgba Gyálcàn, a great master
of the Sagyaba school

$$\left\{ \begin{array}{l} \text{Base (Xí)} \\ \text{Path (Lam)} \\ \text{Fruit (Dràsbu)} \end{array} \right. \quad \rightarrow \quad \textbf{Path} \quad \left\{ \begin{array}{l} \text{View (Dava)} \\ \text{Practice (Gómba)} \\ \text{Attitude (Jyodba)} \end{array} \right.$$

The second aspect of the principal group of three,
the Base, the Path, and the Fruit, is the Path.
Everything in the Path is concerned with how one
can work to bring oneself out of the dualistic
condition, to realization. Because even if the master
has transmitted an Introduction to the primordial
state directly, and has given an explanation of the
state and how it manifests, the problem is that we
ourselves remain closed up in the cage of our
limits. We need a key, a way to open the cage, a
method with which to work to make real what we
have only so far intellectually understood. This key
is the Path, or *Lam* in Tibetan, which itself can be
seen to have three aspects.

Dava: ***Dava: View, or Vision or what is, and how one is***

The first aspect of the Path is the *Dava*, or View. But this is not a philosophical, or intellectual view, such as is meant when people in general use such expressions as 'the View of Nāgārjuna', for example, to describe the Mādhyamika philosophy. This kind of thing is not what is meant by the View in Zógqen at all. What is important in Zógqen is that one really has to observe oneself, and see what one's own condition of body, voice and mind is. Then one discovers exactly how one is conditioned in every sense, and how one is closed up by one's limits in the cage of dualism. This means confronting all one's problems which may not be easy or pleasant. There are many practical problems: of work, of living conditions, getting enough to eat, or actual physical problems. These could be called the problems of the body. Then there are the problems of the voice or energy: nervousness, and other kinds of sickness. But even if we are physically fit and well off materially, there are still the problems of the mind. These mental problems are so many, and can be so subtle and hard to see; there are all kinds of games that we play with our egos. But the result of all this effort is that we build ourselves a cage, without even maybe realizing that we are doing it. So the first thing that has to be done is to discover the cage, and that can only be done by observing oneself all the time. This is another reason why the mirror or meloń is an important symbol in Zógqen. It is not only used to explain the interdependence of the two truths, relative and absolute,[1] but serves as a reminder to observe one's own condition at all times. There is a Tibetan proverb which runs like this:

> On someone else's nose
> one will always notice
> even something so small
> as an ant.

> But on one's own nose
> one won't even see
> something so big
> as a yak

But the Dava of Zógqen means that one doesn't look outwards and criticize others; one observes oneself.

By observing oneself, one can discover one's cage. But then one must really want to come out of the cage. It's not enough just to know about it. The second of the Three Principles of Gárab Dórjé is that, after receiving the Direct Introduction to the primordial state, or Base, one must not 'remain in any doubt', and one can only arrive at this by seeing for oneself, which means observing oneself. This is the real meaning of Dava, or View.

Gómba: actual practices

Yúñdon Dórjébal, a great Zógqen master, was
asked: 'What meditation do you do?'
    He replied: 'What would I meditate on?'
    His questioner asked again: 'So in Zógqen you
don't meditate, then?'
    He replied? 'When am I ever distracted [from
contemplation]?'

The distinction
between
meditation and
contemplation in
the Zógqen
teachings

The distinction between what is meant by the
terms 'meditation', and 'contemplation' in the
Zógqen teachings is an important one. The practice
of Zógqen itself is the practice of contemplation, in
which one abides in that continually self-liberating
non-dual state which is beyond the limits of the
conceptual level of mental activity, and yet which
nevertheless encompasses even the workings of
what is called 'ordinary' mind, or rational thinking.
Although thought can, and does, arise in contemplation, one is not conditioned by it, and it
liberates of itself, just left as it is. In contemplation
the mind is not engaged in any mental effort, and
there is nothing to be done or not done. What is, is
just as it is, self-perfected. What is meant by
'meditation' in the Zógqen teachings, on the other
hand, is one or other of the very many practices
that involve working with the mind in some way,
in order to enable one to enter the state of
contemplation. These practices can include the
various kinds of fixation of the gaze that are done
to bring one to a state of calm, as well as the
various kinds of visualization practices, and so on.
So, in what is called meditation, there is something
to be done with the mind, but in contemplation
there is not.
    In Zógqen contemplation one is able to integrate
either the moment of calm where there is no
thought, or those moments where there is the
movement of thought, equally, remaining in full

Ribga

presence and awareness, neither sleepy nor agitated or distracted. This pure presence, this ground of awareness, neither rejecting nor following thought, is what is meant by the Tibetan term 'rigba', which is the opposite of 'marigba' – the root ignorance of the dualistic mind. If one cannot find this pure presence of rigba, one will never find Zógqen: to find Zógqen, one must bring forth the naked state of rigba. The state of rigba is the pillar of the Zógqen teachings, and it is this state that the master seeks to transmit in the Direct Introduction, the transmission of which, as my master Jyăñqub Dórjé showed me, is not dependent on either formal ritual initiation or intellectual explanation.

But if one does not find oneself dwelling in the state of rigba, it is only by applying the Dava, or View, and by thus observing one's condition at all times that one can know just which practices to work with at any given moment in order to get out of one's cage, and to stay out of it. But if a bird has lived in a cage all its life it may not even know of the possibility of flight; and it has to learn how to fly in a protected situation before it definitively leaves its cage, because without the ability to fly well it will be vulnerable to every kind of predator once the bars of the cage are no longer there to protect it. So, in the same way, a practitioner must develop mastery of his or her energies, and in the Zógqen teachings there are practices to make this mastery possible, practices to suit all kinds of birds and all kinds of cages; but one must know for oneself what kind of bird one is, and what kind of cage one is in. And then, one must really want to come out of all cages, because it's no good just making one's cage a little bigger or more beautiful – by, for example, adding some fascinating new bars made from some 'exotic' Tibetan teaching. It is no good building a new crystal cage out of the Zógqen teachings. However beautiful it might be, it's still a cage, and the whole purpose of the Zógqen teachings is to take one out of all cages into the expanse of the clear sky, into the space of the primordial state.

The Gómba, or practices of the Three Series, can

Principal and
secondary
practices

be classified as either 'principal practices', which are those leading to contemplation, and those of contemplation itself, or as 'secondary practices', which work with contemplation itself in some way, or work to develop some particular capacity. These latter include the practices known as the 'Six Yogas': the practice of inner heat, Dummo, the practice of the transference of consciousness, Pòva (Powa), and so on,[2] as well as all the practices of levels of the teaching other than Zógqen. Sūtra practices, and tantric practices of the paths of purification or transformation may be used, but they are secondary for a Zógqen practitioner.

It must be stressed here that for the practices of Zógqen transmission from a master is essential. The 'secret' of Zógqen is really 'self-secret', since it is open as soon as one can understand it, rather than there being someone who keeps something back as a secret from one. But, nevertheless, some level of commitment is essential on the part of whoever wishes to receive specific instruction in the practices, and ideally there should be a continuing participation between the one who transmits, and the one who receives, until the transmission can be said to be complete. Although there do exist an enormous variety of practices, one does not have to practise every one of them. On the contrary, one uses the practices sparingly as, and when, by observing one's condition, one understands them to be useful or necessary. So we shall only here need to consider enough for a general introductory overview of the Zógqen teachings. But the reader should be aware that a description of a practice is by no means the same as an instruction for practice.

To serve as a key a table of the Three Series appears on p. 80. In general there are practices that work with the body, the voice and the mind. Since each of these has become conditioned, each of these must be worked with. And so, instruction for every practice will usually include the following three elements: what the position of the body should be, how the breathing should be, and what concentration, gaze of the eyes, fixation, or visualization should be done. Some practices are intended to work specifically on one of the aspects of the individual's condition, for example using control of the body and voice to focus the mind. Another practice might be aimed at simply relaxing the body, while another still might work through the voice and sound, like the Song of the Vajra. There are also practices using each of the elements, earth, air, fire, water, and space.

Principal practices of the Three Series of the Zógqen teachings

Semdé: the Series of the Nature of Mind

Lóñde: the Series of Space

Manñagdé: The Essential Series

Four Náljyòr, or Yogas:
(to enable one to enter contemplation)

Four Dá, or Symbols:
(to enable one to enter contemplation)

Four Jogxág: (Jogxág means 'as it is')
(For continuing in Contemplation)
(NB: The Manñagdé also has practices to enable one to enter contemplation: eg.: the Internal and External Ruxan, and the 21 Semzìn.)

1 *Xinás:* 'calm state'; through fixation with an object, and without an object, one arrives at a state of calm. This becomes natural, then stable.

1 *Salva:* 'clarity'; the eyes are open; all one's vision is integrated. This is not the same as intellectual clarity.

2 *Midogba:* 'voidness'; with the open eyes fixed in empty space, unblinking, whatever thought arises, it does not disturb.

1 *Rivo Jogxág:* Jogxág of the mountain; refers to the body. The body is as it is. Whatever the position of the body, that is the position of practice.

2 *Lhagtòñ:* 'more vision', or 'insight'; the state of calm is dissolved, or 'awakened'. One is able to practise with the movement of thought without the effort of maintaining an internal 'watcher'; the state of calm is no longer something constructed.

3 *Déva:* 'blissful sensation'; the body is kept in a controlled position until one is more developed in the practice, yet it is almost as if the body were not there, although one is completely present. Lightly clenching the muscles of the 'lower

2 *Gyácò Jogxág:* Jogxág of the Ocean; refers to the eyes. No particular gaze is needed. Whatever the position of the eyes, that is the position of practice.

3 *Ñísmed:* 'union'; Xinás and Lhagtòñ

3 *Rigba Jogxág:* Jogxág

arise together; one goes beyond duality.

4 *Lhundrub:* 'self perfected'. Non-dual contemplation can be carried into every action. One is fully reintegrated in one's natural condition, and experiences all that arises as the self-perfected play of one's own energy. This is the practice of Zógqen, the Great Perfection.

gates' of the body increases the naturally blissful sensation of complete relaxation.

4 *Yérmed:* 'union'; uniting all the other three Dá carries one into contemplation, and the practice of Zógqen. One keeps the tongue loose in the mouth touching neither roof nor palate, as symbol of this union. All the four Dá are practised together.

of the state; one's state is as it is, without correction. This Jogxág is the same as Lhundrub in the Semdé, and Yérmed in the Loñdé.

4 *Nàñva Jogxág:* Jogxág of vision; all one's vision is said to be 'as an ornament'. One experiences all one's karmic vision as one's own energy, whether as Dáñ, Rolba or Zal. All the four Jogxág are practised together in an instant: Zógqen.

The state of contemplation arrived at is the same in each of the Three Series

Alternative terminology for three aspects of the practice of the Semdé

The terms 'Xinás', 'Lhagtòñ', and 'Ñísmed', belong more properly to the Sutra and Tantra levels of the teachings, but because they are more generally known and used, we have used them here. The terms that are usually found in Zógqen texts for the same phases of practice are: (i) *Násba* (Calm state). (ii) *Miyóva* ('non-movement': from the point of view of pure presence, the movement of thought becomes as non-movement. Thought has power to disturb.) (iii) *Námñid* (equanimity, the state in which all is of the same taste). (iv) Lhundrub, is unchanged: 'self-perfected'.

Furthermore, the term 'Náljyòr', 'yoga' or 'union', could tend to be taken to imply a union of two things, and since there is no notion of a duality to be united in Zógqen, the four phases of practice in the Semdé are simply called the four Dinñezìn, or contemplations.

Each of the Three Series, the Semdé, the Lóñdé, and the Mannagdé, has its own characteristic approach, but the goal is in each case the same: contemplation. And none of the Three Series is a gradual path, because in each case the master transmits directly. But the Mannagdé, which literally means 'secretly spoken series', and which is also called the Ñiñtig, meaning 'heart essence', or 'essence of the essence', is undoubtedly more direct than the Semdé, which works more with oral explanation and detailed analysis. The Mannagdé is extremely paradoxical in its introduction, because the nature of reality does not enter into the limits of logic, and so cannot be explained in any other way than by paradoxes. In the Lóñdé, on the other hand, precise positions of the body and breathing instructions lead the practitioner directly into the experience of contemplation, without the need for intellectual explanations at all [see plates 18-23, and Appendix 3, pp. 159-60].

Although the methods of presentation may vary in the Three Series, there is always a direct introduction in Zógqen. But this does not mean that there is no preparation; rather that the preparation is done according to the needs of the individual. This distinguishes Zógqen from other levels of the path in which there is a hard and fast rule which is the same for everyone. There is no need in Zógqen for certification of one level of attainment or initiation, as is found in the gradual paths, before another higher level can be approached. Zógqen does not work in this way. The disciple is given the opportunity to enter at the highest level right away, and only if the capacity for this level is lacking is it necessary to work down to find a level of practice that will enable whatever difficulties there may be to be overcome so that the disciple can proceed to the level of contemplation itself.

Ñòndrò
Preliminary
Practices

Not only, in all schools of Tibetan Buddhism, does one have to proceed gradually up through all the levels of sūtra and tantra, but before being allowed to practice tantric practices at all, one has to complete a sequence of preliminary practices, or

82

Ñòndrò, which are also known sometimes now-adays as the Four Foundation practices. Their purpose is to develop the capacity of the individual where it is lacking, and it is absolutely correct and traditional that they are a required prerequisite for certain levels of tantric practice. I myself completed the Ñòndrò twice during the course of my education. It is considered compulsory for all who wish to approach the higher practices, in all the four schools.

But Zógqen approaches the situation in another way; its principle is different from that of the tantras. Gárab Dórjé didn't say: 'First teach the Ñòndrò.' He said that the first thing to be done was for the master to give a Direct Introduction; and that the disciple should try to enter into the primordial state, discovering how it is for him or herself, so as to no longer be in any doubt about it; and that then the disciple should try to continue in that state. As and when obstacles arise, the practitioner applies a practice to overcome them. If one finds one lacks a certain capacity, one sets about doing the practice that will help to develop it. Thus one can see that the principle of Zógqen relies on the awareness of the practitioner in deciding what must be done,[3] rather than on a rule compulsorily applied to one and all. This is how it must be in Zógqen.

The Ñòndrò involves practices of Refuge and Bodhicitta, the offering of the Maṇḍala, reciting the mantra of Vajrasattva, and Guru Yoga, all of which must be carried out 100,000 times as a preliminary to receiving higher teachings. Every level of teaching has its value and its principle, and the repetition of these practices as preliminaries truly has its function in relation to the capacity of individuals approaching the tantric teachings. In Zógqen the same practices are carried out; but not as a preliminary to Direct Introduction. They are all undertaken as part of the general daily pattern of practice, and without a requirement to complete a certain specific number of repetitions of them. If the Ñòndrò *is* undertaken as a preparation for tantric practice, then, for it to function, the intention of the practitioner should, in any case, never become merely that of trying to acquire a 'passport' to higher teachings. Such an attitude will surely only bring pride and a false sense of superiority, instead of a deepening of commitment, humility, purification, and devotion to and union of one's mind with that of one's root master. The Ñòndrò exists to enable one to accumulate merit, in order to be able to approach the way of wisdom. If one's intention is not perfect as one carries it out, it will not function.

Tantric practices may be used as secondary practices by the practitioner of Zógqen, alongside the principle practice of contemplation. All tantric practice works with visualization, but in the higher, or Anuttaratantras, the practitioner works to reintegrate his or her dualistic existence into its inherent primordial unity using inner yogic practices as well as visualization. The process of developing the visualization is called 'Gyedrim', and the work with inner yoga is called 'Zógrim', which mean 'Development' and 'Completion' stages respectively. By means of these two stages the impure karmic vision of the individual is transformed into the pure dimension, or 'maṇḍala', of the divinity into whose practice the master has initiated the disciple. Mantra are the natural sounds of the dimension of the divinity, and are recited as the vibrational key to that dimension.

Gyedrim and Zógrim

The word 'Yoga' has now become familiar to most people, but what it brings most readily to mind is the Indian system of spiritual practice known as Hatha Yoga, which is nowadays practised by many people merely as a kind of physical exercise. While it may indeed bring a real benefit even when practised in this way, its primary function is as a spiritual practice. Thus, it is surely important to know at least something about what the aims of the practice are at a spiritual level, and what its philosophical basis is. If Hatha Yoga is well known, it is not so widely appreciated that there is a specifically Tibetan form of Yoga based on the Anuttaratantras. The great pioneer scholar of Western knowledge of Tibetan spiritual tradi-

Yantra Yoga

tions, W.Y. Evans-Wentz, did publish a book in 1958 entitled *Tibetan Yoga and Secret Doctrines* (Oxford University Press, London, 1958), but since he took the Tibetan term 'Trùlkòr', or 'Yantra' in Sanskrit, in only one of its meanings, reading it as a 'geometric diagram of mystical significance', constructed with the intention of enabling the practitioner to 'establish an even more intimate telepathic contact with the deity he invokes', he did not understand that the text he was presenting was actually an instruction in yoga.

'Trùlkòr' in Tibetan, or 'Yantra' in Sanskrit, both mean 'Magic Wheel', and by extension 'engine', or 'machine'. The Sanskrit term 'Yoga' has been translated into Tibetan as 'Náljyòr', a term composed of the noun 'nálma', and the verb 'jyòrba'. 'Nalma' means 'the natural, unaltered state' of anything, and 'jyòrba' means 'to possess'. Thus, if we put the terms 'Trùlkòr' and 'Náljyòr' together, we can see that Yantra Yoga is a method for the individual to arrive at his or her natural state or condition by way of using the human body in the same way as a machine that, once set in motion, produces a specific effect.

While physical yoga has no important role in Hinayāna and Mahāyāna Buddhism, in Tantric Buddhism, also known as the Vajrayāna (Indestructible Vehicle) or Mantrayāna (Mantric Vehicle), it is a fundamental means for realization. But the philosophical basis, methods, and intended results of the yoga of the Vajrayāna are quite different from those of Hatha Yoga. The ultimate aim of Hatha Yoga, as expressed in the Yoga Sūtras of Patanjali, is the dissolution of the vital energy and the complete cessation of all mental activity in a state of union with the absolute, achieved through a path characterized by a gradual neutralization of the body, breathing, senses and mind, and their various functions. The relative is thus regarded as impure, and to be rejected. While this outlook might seem to be similar to that of Hinayāna Buddhism if one confines one's consideration to the concept of Samādhi as cessation (nirodha), it is nevertheless very far from what is aimed at in the

Tantric Buddhism of the Vajrayāna. The fundamental concept behind the yoga of the Anuttaratantra is the recognition of the essential unity of the relative and absolute, a concept already important in the Mahāyāna. But while the Hinayāna and the Mahāyāna sūtra levels both regard the absolute (voidness) as the object of realization, to be attained through freeing oneself from the bonds of the (impure) relative dimension, the tantras begin with the awareness of the voidness of all phenomena (the absolute), and aim at reintegrating it with the relative, working with the method of transformation. The relative is thus not renounced or rejected as impure, but is used as the means of transformation itself, until dualism is overcome, and all phenomena, both relative and absolute, can be said to be 'of one taste' – pure from the very beginning.

Thus in the Yantra Yoga of the Vajrayāna, body, voice, and mind and their functions are not blocked or neutralized, but are accepted as the inherent qualities, or 'ornaments', of the state, manifesting as energy. Since energy is continually in movement, Yantra Yoga, unlike the static Hatha Yoga, is dynamic, and works with a series of movements linked to breathing.

We all have experience of how our emotions and sensations are connected to the way we breathe. A calm, deep, and relaxed regular pattern of breathing accompanies a calm and relaxed state of mind, for example, while a tense, irregular, shallow and rapid breathing pattern accompanies a state dominated by anger or hatred. Thus each mental state has its corresponding pattern of breathing, and Yantra Yoga works with these to regulate the individual's energy, and ultimately to free the mind from conditioning. In many individuals, the body and energy are often so troubled by tensions and disturbances that even if such a person is completely dedicated to working with the mind to enter contemplation, progress is difficult. Yantra Yoga has its function as a secondary practice in Zógqen to overcome such obstacles, and may even help the practitioner overcome physical illnesses, as specific practices of movement linked to breathing are sometimes prescribed by a Tibetan doctor as part of a cure.

It is easy to observe how various positions of the body influence one's breathing pattern. When one is seated with the trunk of the body bent double and thus closed up, the breathing will obviously be completely different from how it is when one is standing with one's arms raised above one's head and one's upper body fully open. To ensure precise control of the breathing, and thus of the energy, Yantra Yoga therefore works with movements that use the possibilities of the various positions in which the body can be placed. What is aimed at is called 'natural breathing', a way of breathing not conditioned by emotional, physical, or environmental factors.

The Inner Maṇḍala

Many tantric divinities are represented as being in union with consorts, and these forms are known as 'Yab-Yum' (father-mother) forms. Their union represents the indissoluble unity of relative and absolute, manifestation and voidness, method and wisdom. They also symbolize the union of what are called the 'solar' and 'lunar' energies, the two poles of subtle energy that flow in the subtle energy system of the human body, which is called the 'Inner Maṇḍala'. When negative and positive circuits are joined in a lighting circuit, a lamp can be lit. When the solar and lunar energies of the subtle energy system of a human being are brought into the state of union which was their inherent, latent condition from the very beginning, the human being can become illuminated. In the same way that, in the Chinese Taoist system of philosophy, Yin and Yang are seen as two principles of energy that are fundamentally inseparable and mutually interdependent constituents of a totally integrated unity, so, too, the solar and lunar energies are seen as fundamentally not-two from the very beginning. Their fundamental unity is symbolized by the Sanskrit syllable 'Evam', which is also a symbol of the Yab-Yum principle.

The Sanskrit syllable 'EVAM' (calligraphy in Tibetan script)

The advanced yogic practice of 'Karmamudrā' ('Action Seal'), which uses sexual union to con-

Karmamudrā

summate the union of the solar and lunar energies, is also a source of the Yab-Yum image as symbol of reality seen as the blissful play of voidness and energy. But Karmamudrā is an actual practice, and not just a fancy way of enjoying sex disguised as spiritual practice. Its importance in the advanced stages of the tantric practice can be understood from the tantric saying: 'Without Karmamudrā, there is no Mahāmudrā.'[4] Karmamudrā is not a principal practice in Zógqen itself. In Zógqen one integrates one's state with whatever experience one encounters, remaining in contemplation, and allowing whatever arises to self-liberate of itself. But the powerful sensation of sexual union, if one does engage in it, is valuable in that its intensity enables one to distinguish clearly the sensation aspect of one's experience from the state of presence, or rigpa, that accompanies it. All sensations are used in this way in Zógqen, and by applying practices that create a variety of sensations, the practitioner is more clearly enabled to distinguish the state of presence, which always remains the same, from the changing sensations. The practices known as the 21 'Semzìn', found in the Zógqen Mannagdé, or Upadeṣa, series, have this particular function, enabling the practitioner to separate the ordinary, reasoning mind from the nature of the mind, which is beyond the intellect.

The Vajra Body

The 'Vajra Body' is the name given to the human body with its Inner Maṇḍala, or subtle energy system, when it is used as a basis for practice to achieve realization. The Inner Maṇḍala has three constituents: Firstly, the body's subtle vital energy in flow linked to the breath, which is called Prāṇa in Sanskrit, and Lún in Tibetan; secondly the subtle currents of prāṇa (Nādi in Sanskrit, Za in Tibetan), some of which flow in actual physical channels, and some of which do not; and thirdly the subtle energy in its essential form, which is called Tigle in Tibetan, and Kundalini or Bindu in Sanskrit. Tigle and lún are not two separate things, the one is the essence of the other. It is the work done with the Inner Mandala that makes the tantric practices of the Path of Transformation a more rapid path to

Amitāyus, the Buddha of Long Life, in union with his consort. Figures shown thus in union are called 'Yab-Yum' (Father-Mother) forms, and symbolize the bliss of realization, the play of energy manifesting from the void, and the essential union of manifestation and voidness. Both Amitāyus and his consort hold, in their right hand, a 'Dàddăr', or arrow with mirror and silk ribbons of five colours, symbolizing the energy of the individual, and in their left hands, a vase of long life.

89

realization than the methods of the sūtras, and there are different types of Yantra connected with the many Mahāyoga tantras and their various Heruka [male wrathful yidam, see p. 38 and plates 4, 7, 9 and 10] practices.

The primary function of Yantra Yoga is to gain mastery of the prāṇa, the vital energy of the body, by means of a series of movements, or Yantra, that are linked to the breathing process to control, coordinate, and develop it; and to activate the tigle, or Kundalini, the vital essence, by means of Asana, or positions linked to movement. It is from the Inner Maṇḍala, or subtle energy system, that the physical body develops. In the process of conception the flow of subtle energy animates and develops the physical foetus in the womb of the mother; thus the correct development of the foetus depends on the proper flow of subtle energy. Similarly, throughout life, the health of a human being depends on the correct circulation of prāṇa and the balance of the elements. A secondary function of Yantra Yoga can therefore be in helping to keep the individual healthy.

Channels and Chakras

According to tantrism there are 72,000 subtle channels in the Inner Maṇḍala; there are main channels, and lesser channels, which branch and interconnect in a pattern like a tree that has a main trunk, with roots and branches spreading out from it into finer and finer configurations. The points where the subtle channels come together, like spokes coming into a hub, are called chakras. There are very many of these, but the principal ones are found along the central channel, which is like the main trunk of the tree in the analogy above. The essence of prāṇa, kundalini or tigle concentrates in these principle chakras, in a subtle channel within the spinal column, called the Gyúñba. At the navel chakra sixty-four channels connect; at the heart chakra eight; at the throat chakra sixteen; and at the head chakra thirty-two.

The central channel or Wúma is flanked by two further major channels to the right and left of it, called Roma and Gyânma, or Solar and Lunar channels, which join it four fingers below the navel and then run parallel to it up the body, arching at the top up over the cranium, before turning down to link up with the right and left nostrils. These three principal channels are shown in the details from the murals from the fifth Dalai Láma's secret temple, to be found among the plates included earlier in this book.

Various tantras give instructions for practice using different numbers of chakras. This does not imply an inconsistency or contradiction; the tantras are in agreement as to the nature of the subtle energy system. But different practices have specific and varying aims. To achieve these aims, different channels and chakras are put into function, and in the description of any given practice only the particular channels and chakras specific to that practice are described. If this is not understood it may seem that the nature of the subtle energy system itself is considered different in different tantras.

Since prāṇa and the mind are linked, prāṇa follows the mind when guided by concentration; prāṇa gathers where the mind focusses it. Similarly the mind can be balanced and integrated through working with the prāṇa, by means of controlled breathing patterns and movements linked to breathing. There are many types of prāṇa, and they support the many types of dualistic mind; as long as the prāṇa circulates in the many and various channels, these dualistic minds persist. But when the prāṇa is brought into the central channel, its essential nature – tigle or kundalini – is activated and enters the channels. Dualistic mind is then overcome, and realization achieved. The vital energy will not normally enter the central channel except at the time of death or during sleep. Only practice will otherwise cause it to do so. Although various tantras specify different chakras at which the prāṇa should be induced to enter the central channel, they all specify that it should be brought to enter there.

There are 108 practices of the 'Union of the Solar and Lunar' Yantra, including: five loosening exercises to prepare the muscles and nerves; five

ཀ྅འ྅ཨཙམ྅ཡུ྅ད྅ངའ྅ཁི྅ལུ྅འ྅ཕྱུ྅ང྅ར྅རུ྅ དྲ྅ག྅ལུ྅ཏ྅ད྅མྐན྅པ྅འི྅སུ྅ལྐ྅ཙྐ྅ཤ྅ག྅ས྅
ར྅བྱུ྅ག྅པ྅བ྅ས྅ བྱུ྅ཙུ྅ཕི྅ན྅ས྅མྐ྅འ྅བ྅ར྅ཕྐ྅ཤྐ྅ནྱུ྅ད྅ར྅ཀྱུ྅ན྅ ཝྐ྅ཏྙ྅ཙྱུ྅ཞྐྷ྅ནི྅ལ྅བ྅ས྅ས྅
ཧྲ྅ཀྐར྅ཙྐྙྀལ྅བྐྣ྅ པྐ྅ ྅

Vairocana

The particular tradition of Yantra Yoga that I teach was
one of the first to be introduced to Tibet. It is connected
with the Heruka Ñónzóg Gyálbo, and known as the
'Union of the Solar and Lunar' Yantra.[5] Its title refers to
the reintegration of the solar and lunar energies of the
subtle energy system. It was written down by Vairocana,
the great Tibetan translator who was a disciple of
Padmasambhava and Hūṃkara,[6] in the eighth century
A.D., and from that time until the present day there has
continued an uninterrupted lineage of transmission of it
until the present day, in Kham, eastern Tibet. It was
summarized and extensively taught by Azòm Drùgba,
from whose direct disciples I received transmission and
instruction.

practices for purification and loosening joints; eight principal movements; five principal groups of five positions; fifty variations on the twenty-five positions; seven lotuses; and the Wave of the Vajra, which corrects all errors of practice.

These 108 practices also include: *the nine purification breathings* which are always practised before a session of Yantra Yoga to expel all the impure air from the system, and are also very beneficial before a session of meditation of any kind; and the *rhythmic breathing* which serves to steady and deepen the breathing, and to develop the capacity for holding the breath which is used in Kumbaka, a particular type of closed holding in which the air is subtly pressed down in the abdominal region, without inflation of the stomach, while at the same time being pulled up from below, to focus and concentrate the prāṇa, before causing it to enter the central channel.

The eight principal movements, or yantra, are a linked series of movements, each of which serves to guide and guarantee a particular type of breathing. By linking the breathing to movement correct timing is guaranteed, and the various positions into which the body is moved ensure that the type of breathing is accurate in each case. The eight types of breathing are as follows: Slow Inhaling; Open Holding; Xíl (or pushing down); Rapid Exhalation; Rapid Inhalation; Closed Holding; Drèn (drawing); and Slow Exhalation. Each of the eight movements have seven phases of breathing. *The five principal groups of five positions*, or Asanas, each work to develop and stabilize a particular aspect of the breathing, combining the eight types of breathing with five methods for causing the prana to enter the central channel. The practitioner does not have to master all of the twenty-five positions, but one from each group is sufficient, depending on the capacity of the individual and the condition of his or her body. Each of the Asanas has seven phases of breathing.

Secondary
Practices

Yantra Yoga is a secondary practice. That is to say, it belongs to the group of practices that help one to approach contemplation, or help one to work with contemplation towards some particular capacity, or to achieve some specific aim, such as healing oneself or others. The reciting of mantras, the visualization of divinities, all the practices of purification, or of transformation, may be used by a practitioner of Zógqen, but their use is secondary to the practice of contemplation. A practitioner of Zógqen is not limited, and can draw from any source that is useful, whenever needed. But, naturally, the practitioner is not in the least interested in making a collection of different paths and traditions, or practices. All one's actions must be governed by awareness, and awareness distinguishes clearly between what is useful, and what is merely distraction.

The Use
of Ritual

People often tell me that they are not interested in ritual practices, only in meditation. But while it is true that ritual practices are secondary to the practice of contemplation in Zógqen, nevertheless, through concentration, mantra and mudrā, a practitioner can have contact with energy in a very real and concrete way. I can show what I mean by this with a story about something that happened during the long journey I made when I left Tibet for India as the political situation in my native country steadily deteriorated and I grew certain that a great upheaval was soon to occur.

I was in a party of four families, about thirty people, travelling with horses from eastern to central Tibet. Because of the presence of the Chinese troops, we didn't make use of the normal roads, but travelled by secondary routes. On these there was further danger from the many bandits who were taking advantage of the confusion of the times to rob groups of travellers. We had many valuable horses, and between the danger from the bandits and the Chinese troops, our journey was very difficult. At a certain point we knew that bandits were on our trail, and we had two skirmishes with them. In the first they succeeded in stealing some of our horses, and in the second we captured two of the bandits. We learned from these two that they were planning to attack us in force, but we didn't know when, and in the middle of the vast plain we were travelling through there was nowhere to hide. I felt that the only thing to do was to summon the help of the Guardians of the teaching, and so whenever we stopped to eat or rest I would go into a little tent, and for hours I would practise a rite invoking them.

The danger increased daily, and a few days later, as I became more deeply involved in this practice, something strange began to happen. I seemed to see sparks coming from the big ritual drum as I sounded it. At first I thought it must be a problem with my eyes, a hallucination, or perhaps some freak of friction between the stick and the drum, but when I called my sister, she too saw the sparks in the air around the drum. Then I called my brother, and later my parents and the whole of our party, and they all saw the sparks. We were sure that it was a sign that the bandits would attack that night, and tied the horses up away from the camp, while everyone stayed awake all night on guard and ready for action. But no bandits came, and when I practised the next day, the sparks were there as before. They continued to manifest day after day for nearly a week as we travelled, but then one day there were no sparks. This time we were certain the bandits would come, and we prepared our defences with great care. Sure enough, we were attacked by a whole band of them. But surprise was on our side, and we were able to drive them off without casualty to our group. From then on they left us alone, and we travelled safely to central Tibet. So you see, even secondary practices can bring very definite advantages!

Guardians of the teaching

There are eight principal classes of Guardians each with many subdivisions. Some are highly realized beings, others not realized at all. Every place, every country, city, mountain, river, lake or forest has its particular dominant energy, or Guardian, as have every year, hour and even minute: these are not highly evolved energies. The various teachings all have energies which have special relationships with them: these are more

ༀ། །བསྐལ་པ་རྡུལ་དང་རྒྱུམ་པའི་དུས་ཀྱི་ལཔར་བོ་རང་། །པསང་དང་ལཔ་ལེན་ཚོ་གས་ཀྱི་རྗེ་མོ་ནི། །མཁོ་འི་དབང་རྒྱུག་གི་དཔའ་པའི་རྒྱུ་མཚོ་ཚ། །ལྲག་གས་དགར་ཡལག་ཆེག་མར་ལྦུ་གང་ཚ་ཟལ་ལོ། །

Ekajati is the principal Guardian of the Zógqen teachings. She manifests as a being with only one of each feature: one eye, one tooth, one tuft of hair, one breast, a personification of the essentially non-dual nature of primordial energy. She is seen dancing on the corpse of the conquered ego, wearing (as Siṃhamukha does) a flayed human skin, and a crown of five skulls representing the five passions that have been overcome and so can be worn as ornaments. She wears a necklace of human skulls, and wields in one hand, as a sceptre, the corpse of a perverter of the teachings. In the other hand she grasps a vanquished demon, and the heart of an enemy. (Tibetan wood-block print.)

ༀ། །ཁྱུང་ཤང་དགྱི་སྲུགས་མ་ཁམ་རཔ་ར་རབབ། ཁྲུབ་དདང་ནོམ་ལྔམ་མྱུ་སྲོ་བམ་རྩུ་དམ་ལྟ། །
བརྩམ་སྲྱ་རྡོ་རྗེ་རབ་གཀ་ལྱེ་ཡུ་ར་མཱ་དང་ སྲོ་ལམ་ཀྱི་དྱེ་ལེ་བན་མ་ར་མུག་ཀ་ཕ་ལ་ཁོ། །

This Tibetan wood-block print shows Dórjé Legba,
another of the principal Guardians of Zógqen, mounted
on a lion. He is also often shown mounted on a goat.
Dórjé Legba, which means 'Good Vajra', was a Bŏn
Guardian and he manifested to oppose
Padmasambhava's efforts to establish the Buddhist
teachings in Tibet. Padmasambhava conquered him and
bound him by oath to protect the teachings. He is thus
sometimes known as the 'Oath-Bound One'. As his
energy is less overwhelming than that of Rāhula, he can
be approached for assistance with relatively mundane
matters, while Ekajati and Rāhula are only concerned
with matters strictly relating to the teachings and
realization.

97

The Guardians of the Mahākāla class are the principal
Guardians of many teachings. They are secondary
Guardians of the Zógqen teachings. There are very many
types of Mahākāla, governed by a principal Mahākāla,
Maniṅ. The mahākālas are male; though there are also
feminine Mahākālis, they are under the dominance of
the Mahākālas. Only the Zógqen teachings, in which the
feminine principle of energy is of such prime
importance, have a feminine protector, Ekajati, as the
principal Guardian.

ༀ། །ཁ་འབར་ཨ་དྲག་པོ་ཡི་ཞི་བར་མཁའ་ནས། ཧྲག་གི་འོད་ཀྱིས་ལག་པ་ཞེ་རས་བ་འཛིན་སོ་ན་ནི། །
དྲག་གར་དྲག་གི་སུགས་གའ་ཞི་སྲུ་འོད་པར་པ། ཁསར་བྲུ་ཏུ་ཁྱག་ཧ་ཊ་ཆེན་པོ་སྲུག་གའ་འཚགས་འཕད། །

Rāhula is another of the principal Guardians of the
Zógqen teachings. His lower body is like that of a snake,
while his upper body is covered with eyes, which,
together with the further eyes in his nine heads
symbolize his ability to see in all directions. His bow and
arrow are ready to strike at enemies, and his many
mouths are ready to devour their ignorance. He is shown
in this wood-block print surrounded by flames of high
energy, as are all Guardians, but Rāhula's power is so
intense that, unless the practitioner has already
developed considerable mastery, he can be a dangerous
ally of potentially overwhelming power if not
approached in the right way.

99

realized Guardians. These energies are icono-
graphically portrayed 'personified' as they were
perceived when they manifested to masters who
had contact with them, and their awesome power
is represented by their terrifyingly ferocious forms,
their many arms and heads, and their ornaments of
the charnel ground. As with all the figures in
tantric iconography, it is not correct to interpret the
figures of the Guardians as 'merely' symbolic, as
some Western writers have been tempted to do.
Though the iconographic forms have been shaped
by the perceptions and culture of those who saw
the original manifestation and by the development
of tradition, actual beings are represented.

Principal Practices

The Semdé practices of Xīnás, involving fixation
to bring one into a state of calm, and Lhagtòn,
enabling one to dissolve the mental activity of
maintaining that state of calm so that one can work
with the arising of thought, are practices of
meditation, rather than of contemplation. They are
nevertheless considered to be principal practices,
as they serve to bring one into contemplation; but
they are not of themselves the actual practice of
Zógqen, because practice becomes truly Zógqen
only when it reaches the level of non-dual contemplation. Indeed practices of Xīnás and Lhagtòn,
though not exactly the same as those found in the
Semdé, are to be found in the Buddhist schools in
general.

Once the state of non-dual contemplation has
been arrived at, by whatever means, from which-
ever of the Three Series, one will have the taste of
it oneself, and one will no longer be in any doubt
as to what it is. Then one must continue in it. This
continuation has two levels of practice, both
principal practices, presented in the Mannagdé.
The Mannagdé is, however, a complete teaching in
itself and has its own secondary practices of
purification and preparation: in the Ruxan which
works to separate the mind from the nature of the
mind; and in the twenty-one principal Semzìn
which work with a whole range of methods,
including fixation, breathing, body positions,
breathing, sound, and so on, to bring one into

Ruxan

The twenty-one principal Semzìn

100

contemplation. Once one has arrived at contemplation through any method, one has to continue in it, and working to bring this continuation into every action and situation is what is called Tregqod, which literally means 'cut loose', in the sense that one relaxes completely in the same way that a bundle of sticks that has been tightly bound together, once the string binding it has been cut, just falls loosely into a more relaxed sort of pattern. Continuing beyond Tregqod there is the practice of Todgál (Togyay), which means 'surpassing the uppermost', with the sense that 'as soon as you're here, you're there'. This practice is genuinely secret, and it is not appropriate to give more than the most basic description of it here. This is not the same as instruction for practice. Todgál is found only in the Zógqen teachings. Through the practice of it one is able to carry one's state of being rapidly to the ultimate goal. By means of the development of the Four Lights, the Four Visions of Todgál arise, and working with the union of vision and emptiness one proceeds until the realization of the Body of Light is attained. This is the consummation of existence, in which the physical body itself is dissolved into the essence of the elements, which is light. We shall discuss this later, when we come to speak of the Fruit, or realization. But for the practice of Todgál to function, the practice of Tregqod must first be perfect, and the practitioner must be able to remain in the state of contemplation at all times.

Although I, for example, had received instructions on the practice of Todgál from Jyăñqub Dórjé when I was with him in Tibet, it was not until many years later that I actually began to put it into practice. I simply did not think that I had developed sufficient capacity. But one night, after I had already been living and teaching at University in Italy for many years, I had a dream. In this dream, as often happened in my dreams, I returned to visit my master Jyăñqub Dórjé in Tibet. On this occasion my master greeted me and said: 'Ah, so you've come back from Italy then, have you?!' 'Yes,' I replied. 'But I have to go back right away.' I was a bit worried about what would happen if the Chinese authorities found me there just like that. Then my master asked me how my practice was progressing. I said that I thought it was going well enough, and he asked: 'What practice have you being doing the most?' 'Still the Tregqod,' I replied. 'Still concentrating on the Tregqod!', he said. '. . . Haven't you begun to practise Todgál yet?' I replied that I hadn't, as he had always told me that it was necessary to become well established in the Tregqod first. 'Yes,' he said, 'but I didn't say that you should spend your whole life practising it; now it's time for you to practise Todgál. If you have any doubts about it, go and ask Jìgmed Líñba.' I thought that this was a very strange thing to say because I knew, of course, that Jìgmed Líñba was a great Zógqen master of the eighteenth century who had been dead for many years. I thought perhaps I had misunderstood what my master had said, so I asked him to explain, but he just said: 'Jìgmed Líñba is up on the mountain behind the house. Go and see him right away.'

Where my master lived there was a high rocky mountain behind his house. He told me that I should climb to the top of this mountain, and that there I would find a cave in which Jìgmed Líñba [see p. 104] would be. But I already knew that mountain well, as while I lived with my master I had climbed it many times to gather medicinal herbs, and then, at least, I had never seen a cave there. So I thought: 'Well that's very strange; I don't think there's a cave there at all', and I asked aloud: 'Which way does one climb up to this cave?', because there were two ways up the mountain. But the master just said: 'Climb straight up from here! Quickly, go on, just do it right away! Ask Jìgmed Líñba to clear up any doubts you may have about Todgál, and then practise it.' Then I couldn't ask any more questions because the master could get quite irascible, and I thought he might scold me if I persisted. So I said: 'Right; I'll go at once', and I set off.

Still dreaming, I climbed up the mountain

directly behind the house. There was no path there, and the rock face was fairly smooth, but I managed to clamber up it. At a certain point I noticed that there were what seemed at first to be mantras carved on the rock, in the way that Tibetans often carve them on such surfaces. Then, when I looked more closely to see what kind of mantras they might be, I saw that they were not really mantras at all. I read a few sentences, and discovered that it was a whole tantra, a tantra of Zógqen it seemed to me. So then I thought: 'This is not a very good action, walking on a tantra!', and I began to recite the 100 syllable mantra of Vajrasattva to purify my negative action, and continued climbing.

Then I arrived at a rock that stood up on end, and on it the title of a tantra was written. I later discovered that it was the name of a derma of the Upadeşa, or Mannagdé series of the Zógqen teachings. I went on climbing beyond this and came to a flat meadow at the far side of which there was a large rocky outcrop. I went slowly towards that, and there, sure enough, I found a cave. Although I wasn't really all that convinced that Jigmed Líñba would be there, I slowly made my way into the cave mouth.

Looking inside, I could see that the cave was fairly large, and that in the middle of it there was quite a big white rock. On this rock there sat a child, a very small young child, who was wearing very light blue transparent clothing, made of a material similar to that from which nightgowns are made in the West. The child had very long hair, and he was sitting quite normally, with his legs stretched out in front of him, not in a meditation or practice position.

I climbed up onto the big white rock, and looked to the left and right to see if anyone else might be there, but there was no one else in the cave. I thought to myself: 'This can't possibly be Jigmed Líñba, because this is only a very young child', and I slowly went nearer to him. The child seemed just as amazed to see me as I was to see him. Then, since my master had specifically sent me to meet

ༀ། །པདྨབྱུང་རྗེ་མེ་འདོན་ཟེ་རསྒྲུསྐ། །རྗེསཔབུ་ནང་ཏི་ཏེ་རུལཛེ་ནཏྲོ་གས། །

དགོངས་མས་ཏེ་རབལྐུན་པབསྤོག་ལབམཟ་རྒྱབྭུ། །ཀུཊྡེ་མེ་སྒྲི་རམལ་སྤུགནར་ཚོས། །

Jìgmed Lìñba (1729–98) was a great Zógqen master of the
Ñiñmaba school who lived in eastern Tibet. He was a
reincarnation of Vimālamitra, the great eighth-century
Zógqen master who became the official teacher of the
Tibetan king Trison Dézan. Jìgmed Líñba brought to
fruition the renaissance of the teachings begun by Lóñqen
Rabjàmba (1308–63), of whom he had many visions
throughout his life. He never undertook any formal
academic studies, but, upon completing a solitary retreat
of five years, manifested such wide knowledge through
his clarity that he came to be universally regarded as a
great scholar. He edited and compiled the Lóñqen Ñìñtig
and left nine volumes of collected works, including
authoritative writings on Tibetan history and medicine,

Jìgmed Líñba and there was no one else in the cave, I decided that this might be him, and that I shouldn't be disrespectful. Thus, as the child still continued just gazing at me, I said with great respect: 'My master has sent me to find you.' The child then, with a sign, but still without speaking, indicated that I should sit down. I thought: 'I wonder what he'll do', and sat down. The child put his hand up to his head, his hair wasn't tied up in any special way, but just hung loose, and he pulled out a piece of rolled up paper a bit like half a cigarette, and opened it. He began reading aloud, and his voice was truly that of a child. It became clear to me that what he was reading was a tantra, and then I thought to myself: 'So there really was something in what my master said when he told me to come up here and find Jìgmed Líñba!', because the words the child was reading were all about the Four Lights of Todgál. I was really amazed, and at that moment I woke up and found myself in my familiar apartment in Italy. I knew then that it was time for me to begin to practise Todgál. Signs of this kind often manifest from one's own clarity when one's master is not present to give instructions or advice in person, but it is important not to confuse fantasy with real clarity. Fantasy is impure vision and arises from karmic traces in the conditioned stream of consciousness of the individual, whereas clarity is a manifestation of pure vision. To begin the practice of Todgál prematurely, or at the wrong time, without sufficient development of Tregqod, will certainly cause serious obstacles on the path. The best safeguard against this is the guidance of a qualified

---

and a text on the curative properties of gem stones when worn next to the skin. He inspired the development of the 'Rismed', or ecumenical, movement that arose in eastern Tibet to draw the various schools of Tibetan Buddhism into a more harmonious collaboration as sectarianism began to divide them.

master, and complete confidence in his instructions on the part of the disciple.

Beginning on the path

Zógqen is considered a very high teaching, containing as it does practices that lead so directly to such complete realization as the Body of Light. Indeed, no one, in any of the Buddhist schools, denies that Zógqen is a high teaching, even the highest. But what they do say, is that it is too high – beyond the capacity of ordinary individuals, and they speak of it almost as if it were only to be practised by realized beings. But, if a being is truly realized, then he or she has no need of a path at all. According to the texts of Zógqen itself, there are just five capacities that someone must have to be able to practise Zógqen, and if one examines oneself and finds that these five are not missing, then nothing is missing. And if any of the capacities is lacking, then one can set about working to develop it. But in most people they will probably already be present.

Five capacities necessary for the practice of Zógqen

1 *Participation:*

This means that one must have a desire to hear and understand the teaching. But more than this, it means that one actively gives one's full cooperation to participating with the master. It is not just that the master explains, and there is nothing required on the part of the disciple.

2 *Diligence:*

This means that one must be consistent in one's participation, and not waver in one's commitment, changing one's mind from day to day, continually putting off doing something.

3 *Present awareness:*

This means that one must not become distracted. One must remain present in the moment, every moment. It is no good knowing all the theory of the teaching, but still living distractedly just the same.

4 *Actual practice:*

One must actually enter into contemplation. It is

not sufficient just to know how to practice, one must actually enter into practice. This is to enter into the Way of Wisdom.

5 *Prajñā:*

Prajñā, in Sanskrit, means literally 'super-knowledge'. Here the sense of it is that one must have sufficient capacity of intelligence to understand what one is taught, and sufficient intuitive capacity to see, and enter into, that which is pointed to beyond the words of the teachings. This is to enter into wisdom itself.

This 'Prajñā' is not of course just an intellectual knowledge. As I have often repeated, my master Jyăṅqub Dórjé, for example, never received an intellectual education; yet his wisdom and the qualities that arose from it were nevertheless quite remarkable. He would sit every day in the enclosed courtyard in front of his house to receive those who came to see him for spiritual or medical advice. He had never actually studied medicine, but his medical knowledge had manifested spontaneously from the great clarity that had arisen from his state of contemplation, and such was his skill as a healer that people came from far and wide to be treated by him. I learned about this clarity at first hand through participating in a process that was another extraordinary manifestation of it.

After I had been only a few days with Jyăṅqub Dórjé, he asked me to take dictation from him. I knew that he could not read and write, and as I can write well enough, I naturally agreed to be of what service I could, without thinking too much of it. I would sit inside the house at a table, and through the one open pane of a window made of four panes of horn I could both see and hear the master outside in the courtyard, where he was usually busy with his patients and disciples. In the middle of all the bustle of activity that surrounded him he would begin to dictate to me, without ever a moment's hesitation about what he was going to say. Then he would stop dictating, all the while carrying on with his work, while I finished writing down what he had said. When I was done, I would

Jyăṅqub Dórjé (Chanchub Dorje)

call out that I'd finished. He would break off talking to those who had come to see him and, without a pause, would begin dictating some more lines, sometimes prose, sometimes verse. But he never once had to ask: 'Now where was I?', 'Where did we stop?', or anything like that. On the contrary, it was often me who had to ask him to repeat something he had said that I had forgotten.

As we proceeded like this for the first few days I was convinced as I was writing that what he was dictating could never possibly hang together. But every night I would go back to my room and read through what I had written down, and I always found that the whole thing flowed along with a complete continuity just like a perfectly conceived and written intellectual text; this is in fact exactly the way in which 'Gónder' [mind derma] always manifests. Over the next weeks we completed a big volume working in this way, and I later saw some of the twenty other such volumes that had been similarly dictated to his other disciples.

The author's principal master, Jyáñqub Dórjé, is shown here seated in the enclosed courtyard of his house in Dégé, eastern Tibet, waiting to receive patients or other visitors. He wears the robes of a layman and a traditional *melôn*, a mirror made of five precious metals, symbol of Zógqen, on a cord around his neck. On the table in front of him are small bags of medicine, a measuring spoon and medicine bowl. Behind him, to the right, are two larger sacks of medicine, and above them, glimpsed through the open window, the author sits at a table inside, ready to take dictation. Prayer flags flutter above. The story represented in this contemporary line drawing by Nigel Wellings is told on p. 107.

All that arises
is essentially no more real
than a reflection,
transparently pure and clear,
beyond all definition
or logical explanation.

Yet the seeds of past action,
karma, continue to cause
further arising.

Even so –
know that all that exists
is ultimately void of self-nature
utterly non-dual!

These words of the Buddha are a perfect explanation of Zógqen

$$
\left\{
\begin{array}{l}
\text{Base} \\
\text{Path} \\
\text{Fruit}
\end{array}
\right.
\quad \rightarrow \quad \textbf{\textit{Path:}} \quad
\left\{
\begin{array}{l}
\text{Dava} \\
\text{Gómba} \\
\text{Jyodba}
\end{array}
\right.
$$

JYODBA: Conduct, or Attitude

The last of the three aspects of the Path, is *Jyodba*, which means 'Conduct', or 'Attitude', and this is a very important aspect of Zógqen, because this is the way practice is brought into daily life so that there is no separation between practice and whatever activity one engages in. Until one is able to live in contemplation, in the self-perfected state, in which one finally self-liberates like a snake unwinding of itself, it is necessary to govern one's attitude with awareness, and train oneself not to become distracted. We have already seen that present awareness is one of the five capacities necessary to practice Zógqen; one must really be present and mindful in every moment.

The Zógqen practitioner can use this present awareness in daily life so that what would otherwise be the 'poison' of dualistic experience itself becomes the path to remain in contemplation and to go beyond dualism. In the same way that flowing water freezes into solid ice, the free flow of primordial energy is solidified by the action of conditioned cause and effect, the functioning of the individual's karma, into a seemingly concrete material world. The 'great perfection' of the practitioner's attitude, or Jyodba, makes possible the mastery of karmic causes, so that they self-liberate as they arise.

Primary and secondary karmic causes

Primary karmic causes, good or bad, are like seeds which are capable of reproducing the species of plant from which they came. But just as seeds need secondary causes such as light, moisture, and air if they are to mature, so too do the primary karmic causes, remaining as the traces of past actions in the stream of consciousness of the individual, need secondary causes if they are to be able to mature into further actions or situations of the same kind. By means of continual awareness the practitioner can work with the secondary causes arising as the conditions he or she encounters in daily life, so that negative primary causes are prevented from coming to fruition, at the same time as positive primary causes are furthered, finally arriving at a state where it is possible to avoid being conditioned by any experience that arises, good or bad, and achieving complete liberation from conditioned existence altogether. For any action of body, voice, or mind to become a perfect primary karmic cause capable of conditioning the individual and producing a full karmic consequence, all these three aspects must occur: first there must be an intention to act; then the action itself; and finally, there must be satisfaction at having performed the action.

Three factors necessary to produce a primary karmic cause

A practitioner can develop beyond the dualistic level of conditioned karma that divides things into good and bad, and may thus be able to do all kinds of things that seem outrageous from the divisive dualistic point of view of ordinary karmic vision. This doesn't mean, however, that everyone who practises Zógqen must live like the famous Tibetan crazy-wisdom yogi, Drùgba Gunlegs (Drukpa Kunley),[7] of whom so many interesting stories are told, many of them hilariously bawdy. He was beyond dualism, and someone who is truly beyond all limits doesn't behave as others expect. But this is not the same at all as being distracted. There is all the difference in the world between Zógqen, the Great Perfection, the practice of non-dual contemplation manifesting as a spontaneous life lived enjoying the play of one's own energies, and living in a completely distracted way. Zógqen is not mere licence, and so awareness must be present at all times. But, then again, this is not the same as living by the rules. Awareness is the only rule in Zógqen. Or, perhaps it would be better to say that awareness replaces all rules in Zógqen, because a Zógqen practitioner never either forces himself to do anything, nor submits to being conditioned by anything 'external'.

This doesn't mean that a Zógqen practitioner shows no respect for the rules that other people live by. One doesn't just go around being contrary to everyone else, and using Zógqen to justify one's own actions. Awareness means one is aware of everything, including the needs of other people. And even if the Absolute condition exists, beyond the level of good and bad, the relative condition nevertheless still continues to exist for us as long as we remain bound by dualism, so we have to be aware of that, too. But we can live respecting the conditions which exist around us without getting bound up in them. This is what awareness means, and this is the principle of the attitude or *Jyodba*, of a Zógqen practitioner.

One must not become conditioned by the teachings themselves. The teachings are there to make one more independent, not more dependent. So a Zógqen master will always be trying to help the disciple to become more truly autonomous, to come out of all cages, completely. And thus, while the master is certainly able, out of his or her greater clarity, to give advice to disciples, even on quite detailed matters relating to everyday life, he or she will always be trying to help them to observe themselves, and to make decisions out of their awareness.

Masters can, of course, just as well be women as men. When I was fourteen, I myself spent two months with the great woman master Ayu Kàdro who lived a few days' ride away from my college. As she was considered to have realized the practice of Vajrayogini, and thus to be an embodiment of this Dākinī, I was sent during a break in my college studies to ask her for the Vajrayogini initiation. She was a very aged woman, not at all well known, who had lived for more than fifty years in a small house in total darkness working with a practice known as the 'Yañtig' which enables someone who is already able to remain in the state of contemplation to proceed to total realization through the development of inner luminosity and visionary clarity.

Yañtig

When I arrived at Ayu Kàdro's house it became clear that she could see as well in the dark as she could in the light. Although her attendant lit a few butter lamps for my benefit, I was aware that Ayu Kàdro herself had no need of them. By the light of the lamps I saw the features of this very striking old woman. Her long hair, which hung down well below her waist in plaited braids, was grey from its roots to below her shoulders, but from there on it was black to its tips. It had clearly never been cut.

At first Ayu Kàdro declined to give me the initiation I requested, saying she was just a poor old woman who knew nothing about the teachings, but she did suggest that we camp nearby for the night. During the night she had an auspicious dream in which her master urged her to give me the initiation, and so, in the morning she sent her attendant with breakfast for my mother and sister, and an invitation for me to go to see her. In the following weeks she transmitted a great deal of teaching to me, including the complete practice of the Yaṅtig, and I regard her as one of my principal masters. During my stay with her, in response to my questions, she told me her life story, which I later wrote down.[8]

So, the Jyodba, or conduct of a Zógqen practitioner means that one stays present in awareness in every moment, and doesn't let one's mind wander following the stream of thoughts about the past, worries about the present, or plans for the future. It's not that one doesn't plan: one remains mindful of secondary causes as they arise, and relates to them without neurosis, unlike the father of Famous Moon, who is the unfortunate hero of a Tibetan folk tale that illustrates very well the kind of thing that's likely to happen when one doesn't stay present.

The story tells that there was once a man so poor that the only way he could get something to eat was to go from door to door asking others more fortunate than himself to give him some grain. One day he was lucky; he received a great deal of grain, and he went home happy. His house was very small indeed, and since there were so many mice in it, he decided to hang his precious grain in a sack suspended by a rope from the roof beam, so that the mice couldn't get at it. Then he lay down for the night on his bed, which was below the sack, there being so little room in the house. He couldn't get to sleep right away, so he began to make plans in his mind. He thought to himself: 'I won't eat all the grain in my sack; I'll save some of it for seed, plant it, and then grow more grain. In a year I'll have ten sacks, and the year after that I'll have a hundred.' And he went on planning how year after year he'd have more sacks until he was rich, and then he thought: 'I won't have to live in this tiny little hut any more, I'll build myself a palace and have servants to look after me. I'll find myself a beautiful wife, and then of course we'll have children. We'll have a son first, I'm sure, but what on earth shall we call him?' And he lay there trying to think of a name for his future son. He thought of many names, but none of them pleased him. Finally, a clear bright moon rose in the black sky, and as soon as he saw it he exclaimed to himself: 'That's it! I'll call him Famous Moon!', but at that precise moment the mouse that had been gnawing at the rope that held the sack of grain tied to the beam above him finally cut through the rope with his teeth, and the sack fell on the poor man's head, killing him instantaneously, so that none of his elaborate plans ever came to be. Living in dreams of the future even the present escaped him.

CHAPTER 8

The Fruit

If the intention is good,
the Path and the Fruit
will be good.
If the intention is bad,
the Path and the Fruit
will be bad.
Since everything thus depends
on a good intention,
always strive to cultivate
such a positive mental attitude.

Jìgmed Líñba

Base
Path
Fruit → **THE FRUIT, or REALIZATION**

The
Gákyìl

The divisions of the teaching of Zógqen are for the purposes of explanation only. To become realized means that one makes real that which was one's condition from the beginning, the Xí, or Base. Realization is not something that has to be constructed. It is one's inherent condition from the very beginning. And in Zógqen, in particular, since it is not a gradual method, the Path is precisely to enter the primordial state, which is both the Base, and the Fruit. This is why the Gákyìl, the symbol of primordial energy, which is a particular symbol of the Zógqen teachings, has three parts which spiral in a way that makes them fundamentally one. The Gákyìl, or 'Wheel of Joy', can clearly be seen to reflect the union and interdependence of all the groups of three in the Zógqen teachings, but perhaps most particularly it shows the interconnection of the Base, the Path and the Fruit. And since Zógqen, the Great Perfection, is essentially the self-perfected unity of the primordial state, it naturally requires a non-dual symbol to represent it.

Sèva
Mixing

So the Path is not strictly separate from the Fruit, rather the process of self-liberation deepens until it reaches the Base that has existed from the beginning, and reaching this is the Fruit. The Tibetan word *sèva*, which means 'to mix', is used here: one mixes one's contemplation with every action as one lives one's ordinary life. There is nothing to change in Zógqen, no special clothes to be worn, and nothing to be seen from the outside. There is no way to know if someone is really practising or not. The practice is absolutely not dependent on outward form. But the principle is that everything in one's relative situation can be brought into practice and integrated. Of course, this means that one's contemplation must be precise, or there would be nothing to mix, and this is what is meant by the second of Gárab Dórjé's Three Principles, 'not remaining in doubt'. There's no doubt about what contemplation is, it's precise.

Jerdröl,
Xardröl,
and Rañdröl

Then the three capacities of *Jerdröl*, *Xardröl*, and *Rañdröl* are developed. The '*dröl*' part of the name, in each case, means 'Liberation', as in the name of the famous Bărdo Tosdröl, which is translated as 'Liberation through hearing in the state of the Bărdo', but which is better known nowadays as 'The Tibetan Book of the Dead'. In *Jerdröl*, the first of the three, the process of self-liberation is still at a minor capacity.

Jerdröl

Jerdröl means: 'one observes and it liberates', and the example given is of the way a dewdrop melts when the sun shines on it. But the sun, in this example, shouldn't be seen as implying that in Zógqen, some sort of antidote is needed to deal with the poison of dualism. It's just that one's awareness is always maintained, and kept constantly present, and whatever arises self-liberates.

Xadröl

Xadröl is a medium capacity, and it is illustrated by the image of snow melting as it falls into the sea. The snow here represents sense contacts, or passions, and *Xadröl* means 'as soon as it arises it liberates'. So as soon as there is any kind of sense contact, it liberates of itself, without even any effort to maintain awareness. Even passions that would condition someone who has not reached this level of practice can simply be left as they are. This is why it is said that all one's passions, all one's karmic vision, become just like ornaments in Zógqen, because without being conditioned by them; without being attached to them, one simply enjoys them as the play of one's own energy, which is what they are. This is why certain tantric divinities wear, as an ornament, a crown of five skulls which represent the five passions that have been overcome.

Rañdröl

The final capacity of self-liberation is called *Rañdröl*, which means 'Of itself it liberates itself', and the example used is that of the speed and ease of a snake unwinding its own coils of itself. This is completely non-dual and all-at-once, instantaneous self-liberation. Here the separation of subject and object collapses of itself, and one's habitual vision, the limited cage, the trap of ego, opens out into the spacious vision of what is. The bird is free, and can finally fly without hindrance. One can enter and enjoy the dance and play of energies, without limit. The development of this vision is said to spread like a forest fire, until the sense of a subject subsides of its own accord. One experiences the primordial wisdom in which, as soon as an object appears, one recognizes its emptiness as being the same as the voidness of one's own state. The union of emptiness and vision, and the presence of the state and emptiness are all experienced together. Then everything can be said to be 'of one taste', which is the emptiness of both subject and object. Dualism is completely overcome. It's not that subject and object don't exist, rather that there is the continual presence of contemplation, and through the practice of self-liberation, one does not remain limited by dualism. This is the state pointed to in the last of the Six Vajra Verses:

> Seeing that everything is self-perfected
>   from the very beginning
> the disease of striving for any achievement
>   is surrendered
> and just remaining in the natural state
>   as it is,
> the presence of non-dual contemplation
>   continuously spontaneously arises.

The interdependence of subject and object: how the senses maintain the illusion of dualism

Now, as this experience deepens towards realization, certain capacities may begin to manifest. But to understand these capacities at all, one must understand how the illusion of dualism is maintained by the subject-object polarity of the senses, which is analysed as the six sense subjects and the six sense objects. This means that, for example, the capacity for seeing arises interdependently with what is perceived as visual form, and the perception of visual form arises together with the capacity for seeing. This analysis can be carried on right through the various senses, hearing and sound arising together, and so on, until the last of the six, which is considered to be the interdependent arising of mind and existence, the interdependent arising of mind and what one experiences as one's reality. Through an understanding of this interdependent arising of each sense and its respective object, one can understand how the illusion of duality is self-maintaining, subject implicitly implying object, and object implicitly implying subject, in the case of each sense, until finally, all the senses, including the mind, together create the illusion of an external world separate from a perceiving subject. But the best way to understand this is by observing oneself, and watching one's own mind, in practice, and seeing how thoughts arise like waves, and how one's senses function in relation to one's sense of a self.

As Śākyamuni Buddha himself said:

> To enter contemplation for the time
> it takes for an ant to walk from

one end of one's nose to the other,
will bring more progress towards realization
than a whole lifetime spent in the accumulation
of good actions [merit].

The
Five
Ñónxes

With the advancing of the practice, all thoughts, and indeed all the sensations of all the senses, self-liberate. The illusion of dualism is undone, and then t'irough the re-unification of subject and object, the five Ñónxes, five 'higher forms of awareness' may manifest in the practitioner. These are not to be sought in themselves. They must arise, as tne practice progresses, as a by-product of it, and they must not be taken as its goal.

The first of these is of the eyes, vision. It is called 'real knowledge of the eyes of the divinities', because we usually think of divinities as beings with a greater capacity than ours. What it means is that one develops the capacity, for example, to see things regardless of distance. One can even see things when they are behind other objects that are in the way of our 'normal' vision.

Then there is a similar capacity with regard to hearing – the 'real knowledge of hearing', or 'hearing with the ears of the divinities'. One is able to hear all sounds, regardless of distance, whether they are loud, or soft, and so on.

The third capacity is the knowledge of the minds of others, in other words, being able to read other people's thoughts. The individual is made up of body, voice, and mind. What one sees with the eyes is basically physical form or body, while the capacity for hearing is related to the voice, energy, sound. Body and voice are more concrete than the mind, and so it is easier to gain the capacities relating to them. It is very difficult to know, or to understand, exactly what another person is thinking. But it is a capacity that can arise.

There is a rather humorous story of my master Jyăñqub Dórjé's clarity that illustrates these kinds of capacities well. As I have already said, Jyăñqub Dórjé practised as a doctor, and when he had successfully cured a certain well-off patient who lived several days' journey away, that patient decided to send a servant with a gift to the master by way of thanks. The servant set out on horseback bearing the gift, which was a wrapped parcel tied with string, containing within it many smaller packets of tea. The servant rode all day, but when he stopped for the night, still two days' ride away from Jyăñqub Dórjé's home, he decided that the master wouldn't miss a few of the packets of tea. So, pulling out his knife, he cut open the package and removed one third of them. Then he resealed and tied the now smaller parcel, so that it looked perfect, as if it had never been opened.

I was at Jyăñqub Dórjé's house two days later when the master, right out of the blue, suddenly asked his wife to prepare a meal for someone who would presently arrive. Everyone in Jyăñqub Dórjé's community was used to events that would seem strange elsewhere, and so, without question, the master's wife began to do as she was asked. Her husband requested that the meal be formally laid out with all the necessary plates and cutlery, but specifically insisted that no knife should be provided. All this was the more unusual because, unless the expected visitor was a very important person of some kind, he or she would not normally eat separately from everyone else.

When the servant messenger at last arrived, I watched very carefully to see what would happen. He greeted the master with great respect, presenting the sealed parcel to him and conveying the thanks of his employer who had been cured. Jyăñqub Dórjé thanked him in return, put the parcel aside saying he would open it later, and asked the messenger if he was hungry. When the latter replied that he was, the meal that had been prepared was served to him. The meal was a little more lavish than was usual for us, and included several courses, which the messenger ate with relish. When he came to the meat course, however, he noticed that there was no knife on the table with which to cut the meat. He had just begun to seek the knife from the scabbard hidden in the folds of his clothes, when the master fixed him with a fierce gaze and said quietly: 'It's no good searching for your knife in there, my friend. You left it on the boulder beside the road two nights ago when you used it to open the parcel intended for me and stole one third of the packets of tea!' You can perhaps understand from this why no one in Jyăñqub Dórjé's community either lied or tried to practice any deception.

The fourth capacity that may manifest on the path to realization is the knowledge of life and death. One can know, for example, when someone is going to die, in what way, and where they will be reborn. The principle of this is the development of the capacity to know time to the point of being able to go beyond time. One develops the capacity to know all the secondary causes relating to another person. The secondary causes [primary and secondary karmic causes, see p. 111] that will manifest when that person dies are actually present in any given moment, and so can be read.

As an illustration of this capacity there is another story of a servant coming as a messenger to Jyăñqub Dórjé. This man was sent by his employer, who once again lived several days' ride away, to ask for some medicine for his daughter who was seriously ill. Jyăñqub Dórjé, however, said that medicine would be of no use, as the daughter had died just after the messenger had set out to come to him, a fact that he could not have known except through his clarity. The messenger did not know whether to believe him or not, and returned home at once with medicine lest the girl should indeed still be alive, in which case his employer would say he had failed in his duty. But when he arrived home he found that the daughter had died at exactly the time Jyăñqub Dórjé had said.

The fifth capacity is called 'real knowledge of miracles'; and this is not just an intellectual understanding, but the actual concrete capacity to perform miracles. One has gone beyond all limits, and in that state such activity becomes natural rather than really miraculous at all. Miracles are usually thought of as actions someone might perform in relation to seemingly external objects, changing them in some way. But, as the division of reality into internal and external is an illusion, when that illusion is overcome it is possible to go beyond all usual limits with one's own being, as the great yogi Milarasba did, when he sheltered from a hailstorm by actually getting inside a yak's horn that was lying on the ground. [See plate 25.] It is said that neither did the yak's horn get bigger, nor Milarasba smaller. Another insight into the reality beyond our usual limits can be gained from the Buddha's statement that there are as many Buddhas in an atom as there are atoms in the universe. We just can't get at the meaning of such a statement within our usual framework of mental concepts, so we call such things miraculous; but this is how reality is – only we're not used to seeing it as it is. When someone actually develops the capacity to enter into what is, this is called 'the real knowledge of miracles'.

Total Integration of Subject and Object

So this is how the signs of the Path may develop for a practitioner, though they may not arise in any particular order. But now we come to a sixth capacity, a capacity of the Fruit, which is called Sprosbal, meaning 'beyond concept', or 'like the sky'. This involves the complete re-integration of subject and object, and is a particular Zógqen method of attaining Total Realization in one lifetime, through the mastery of one's energy and the way that it manifests.

All the methods of the various paths, those of the sūtras and all the levels of tantra, as well as those of Zógqen, lead to Total Realization – the Fruit. This is complete liberation from conditioned existence in a state of being with absolute mastery of all the phenomena of reality and omniscient perfect wisdom in every capacity. But the sūtras explain that their methods require many kalpas, or aeons, to reach this state; and even though the methods of the lower tantras are quicker, they too require many lifetimes. The higher tantras and Zógqen both enable one to reach Total Realization in one lifetime, but the methods of Zógqen are more direct even than those of the higher tantras. The realization of the visions of the Lóñdé, or of the practice of Todgál – the ultimate, secret teaching of Zógqen – enable the practitioner to rapidly undo the knots of conditioned existence, and as a function of the Total Realization thus arrived at, the physical body dissolves into the essence of its elements, which is light.

Internal Yíñ and External Yíñ

To accomplish this realization, 'Semñid', which means the 'nature of the mind', also called the 'internal yíñ', is integrated with 'Qosñid', which means the 'condition of existence', also called the 'external yíñ'. That they are both called 'yíñ' (meaning 'space'; dhatu in Sanskrit) shows that from the beginning they are of the same nature. It is not that existence is cancelled out in some way: rather that, from the point of view of Zógqen, the individual can always be said to be the centre of the universe, in the sense that the individual as microcosm is a perfect reflection of the universe as macrocosm. The essential nature of the one is the essential nature of the other. When one realizes oneself, one realizes the essential nature of the universe. The existence of duality is only an illusion and when the illusion is undone, the primordial unity of one's own nature and the nature of the universe is realized, or made real. Through the integration of the internal yíñ and the external yíñ one manifests the Body of Light. If the other five Nõnxes were signs of the development on the Path, this is finally the Fruit.

The Body of Light

The Jàlus (in Tibetan) or Body of Light realized through the practice of Zógqen is different from the 'Jyulus', the 'Mayic' or 'Illusory' Body realized through the practices of the Higher Tantras. The Jyulus is dependent on the subtle prāṇa of the individual, and thus, since prāṇa is always considered to be of the relative dimension in Zógqen, this Jyulus is not considered to be Total Realization. The Jàlus, or Body of Light, itself, is a favourite mode of realization manifested by the masters of

124

both the Lóñdé and the Maññagdé, and with only
very short breaks in the lineage, it has continued to
be manifested right up to the present day. The
master of my master Jyáñqub Dórjé achieved this
level of realization. Jyáñqub Dórjé was present at
the time, so I know it is not a fable. My master told
me how his master Ñaglà Padma Dúddùl called all
his disciples together, those who were farther away
as well as those who were close at hand, and told
them he wanted to transmit some teachings that he
had until then not given them in full. So he
transmitted these teachings, and then they practised a Gana Puja together for more than a week.
Gana Puja is an excellent way of eliminating
disturbances between master and disciple and
between disciple and disciple. Then, at the end of
that week. Ñaglà Padma Dúddùl announced to
them that it was time for him to die, and that he
intended to do so on a certain mountain nearby.
His disciples implored him not to die, but he said
that it was time, and that there was nothing to be
done about it. So they all accompanied him up the
mountain, to a place where he set up a little tent.
Then he had his disciples sew the tent up
completely, sealing him inside it, and he asked to
be left in peace for seven days.

The disciples went down the mountain, and
waited camped at the foot of it for seven days,
during which time it rained a great deal and there
were many rainbows. Then they went back up and
opened the tent, which was sewn up just as they
had left it. All that they found inside was the
master's clothes, his hair, and his nails. His clothes
were the clothes of a lay person, and they
remained there in a heap where he had been
sitting, with the belt still wrapped around the
middle. He had left them just like a snake sheds a
skin. My master was present, and told me this
story, so I know that it is true and that such
realization is possible.

I know many other such stories, but there is a
particularly interesting one that my uncle Dogdán
told me. In 1952, in the area of Tibet that I come
from, there lived an old man who, when he was

125

young, had been a kind of servant or assistant to a Zógqen master for a few years, and thus naturally had heard many teachings. But for the rest of his life he had just lived very simply, cutting mantras into stones for a living. He lived in this way for many years, and no one took much notice of him, or thought he was a practitioner. But then one day he announced that he was going to die in seven days time, and sent a message to his son, who was a monk, saying that he wanted to leave all his possessions as an offering to the monastery where his son lived. The monastery spread the news far and wide that this man had said that he wanted to be left closed up for seven days to die, and since everyone understood the significance of this, many people came, and the whole thing became a public event. There were representatives of all the various Buddhist schools, from the great monasteries, and even members of the Chinese administration, who at that time were all military personnel. Thus, when they opened the room in which the man had been locked for seven days, there were many people present. And what they saw was that the man had left no body. Only his hair and nails, the impurities of the body, were left.

My uncle, the yogi, came to see me at my father's house just after he had witnessed this event, and his eyes were full of tears as he told me about it. He said it was a terrible tragedy that none of us had known enough to recognize that this seemingly ordinary person, living so close to us, had actually been a very great practitioner, from whom we could have received teaching. But this is how it is with practitioners of Zógqen. There is nothing to be seen on the outside.

When I visited Nepal in the spring of this year (1984) to give teachings and to practise at Tolu Gónba, a mountain monastery close to the Tibetan border, near Mount Everest, where Padmasambhava practised, and at the cave of Maratika where Padmasambhava and his consort Mandarava realized the practice of long life, I had news of what became of my uncle Dogdán. This news came from a Tibetan who had just arrived in Kathmandu from Tibet, where he had been a government official in the region where Dogdán lived. It seems that my uncle continued to live in his isolated cave in retreat for many years after I left Tibet, but eventually, like many other similar yogis, he was made to come out of retreat in the period of the Cultural Revolution, when it was decreed that such persons were exploiters of the workers because they were provided with food although they did not work. He was more fortunate than many others, and was only placed under house arrest, rather than having to face a public trial and possible serious punishment. The man I met in Kathmandu had, among many other responsibilities, been responsible for the continuing custody of Dogdán, whom he allowed to live in a small wooden house built on the flat roof of an ordinary town house in the provincial capital, belonging to a Tibetan family who provided for my uncle's needs, so that he was able to continue his retreat as before. Later, because this official vouched for him, he was allowed to go and live in the country under less strict supervision. He was allocated an isolated house to live in, and the official regularly visited him there to check up on him.

But, one day, the official arrived and found the house closed up. When he managed to get in, he found Dogdán's body on his meditation couch; but the body had shrunk to the size of that of a small child. The official was very worried: how was he to explain such a thing to his Chinese superiors. He was afraid they would probably believe that he was aiding Dogdán's escape in some way, and so he went at once to inform them of what had happened. When he returned to the isolated house a few days later with all the high ranking officers of the regional government, Dogdán's body had disappeared completely. Only the hair and the fingernails were left. When his superiors bewilderedly asked for an explanation, the Tibetan official could only say that he had heard that ancient religious texts spoke about yogis realizing what was called a 'Body of Light', but that he had never expected to see such a thing. The event made such an impression on him that he developed a strong interest in spiritual matters, and as soon as he could, managed to escape on foot into Nepal where he felt he would be free to receive teachings and practice, and where I met him. I was deeply moved to hear of my uncle's realization. Knowing how serious a problem he had had with mental illness in his early life, I did not expect him to achieve so much in one lifetime. His example shows what is possible for every individual.

The Way of Light

To use the metaphor of the mirror once again, this realization of the Body of Light means that one is no longer in the condition of the reflections, but has entered the condition of the mirror itself, and moved into the nature and energy of the mirror. Knowing how one's own energy manifests as *Dáñ*, *Rolba*, and *Zal*, one is able to integrate one's energy completely, right through to the level of actual material existence. This is accomplished either through the visions of the Lóñdé that arise as a result of the practices of the four Dá; or through the practice of the Four Lights that bring about the arising of the Four Visions of Todgál. These develop very much as the visions of the Lóñdé develop. The first of these is called the 'Vision of Dharmata' (or 'essence of reality'), and the second vision is the further development of the first. The third is the maturation of it, and the fourth is the consummation of existence. If, while alive, one has entered the third level of these visions – and to say one has 'entered' means that there are certain signs that this is so – then, when one dies, one's body slowly disappears into light. Instead of decomposing into its constituent elements in the usual way, it dissolves into the essence of its elements, which is light. The process may take longer than seven days to happen. This is the realization that masters such as Gárab Dórjé achieved. All that remains of the physical body are the hair and finger nails, which are considered to be its impurities. The rest of the body has dissolved into the essence of its elements.

A practitioner who manifests this realization cannot really be said to have 'died', at all, in the ordinary sense of the word, because he, or she, still remains *active* as a principle of being, in a Body of Light. The activity of such a being will be directed for the benefit of others, and such a being is actually visible to someone in a physical body who has sufficient clarity.

The Great
Transfer

But a practitioner who perfects and completes the fourth level of the Todgál visions does not manifest death at all, and makes this transubstantiation while actually living, with none of the symptoms or phenomena of a physical death, gradually becoming invisible to someone with normal karmic vision. This level of realization is called the 'Great Transfer', and this is the realization that Padmasambhava and Vimālamitra manifested. Both the Great Transfer and the Body of Light are in essence the same; it is just that, in the Great Transfer, one arrives earlier. These two modes of realization are particular to the practice of Zógqen.

Total realization

The THREE
BODIES
Nirmāṇakāya,
Sambhogakāya,
and Dharmakāya

Ordinary beings are reborn without choice, conditioned by their karma into taking a body according to the causes they have accumulated over countless past lives. A totally realized being, on the other hand, is free from the cycle of conditioned cause and effect. But such a being may manifest a body for the purpose of helping others. The Body of Light, or the Light Body of a being who has realized the Great Transfer, are both phenomena which can be *actively* maintained for the purpose of communicating with those who have sufficient visionary clarity to be able to perceive such a body. But to help those who lack such capacity, a totally realized being may manifest in an actual physical body as, for example, Gárab Dórjé and the Buddha did. All these kinds of bodies are of the Nirmāṇakāya: *kāya*, in Sanskrit, means 'body', or 'dimension', and *nirmāṇa* means 'manifestation'. So a totally realized being may choose to manifest a Body of

Light, or voluntarily take a rebirth in an ordinary physical body in the gross material dimension, but is not conditioned by such a body, or by the actions carried out in it.

The Sambhogakāya, or 'Body of Wealth', is the dimension of the essence of the elements that make up the gross material world, a subtle dimension of light appearing in a wealth of forms which can only be perceived through the development of visionary capacity and mental clarity. A totally realized being may manifest a Sambhogakāya form, but in such a form is *not* active as is a being who manifests in a Body of Light.

Just as the rays of the sun are a manifestation of its inherent qualities, so too the wisdom of a totally realized being *is* what that being is. Each Sambhogakāya form is a 'personification' of a principle of pure wisdom. But just as the sun does not intend to send its rays to any particular place, and it depends on the characteristics of the place as to whether it will receive the rays, it is the practitioner who must be active to perceive the dimension of the Sambhogakāya and gain access to the wisdom personified by a particular Sambhogakāya form, opening that dimension of his or her own being.

Although the capacity to manifest either Sambhogakāya or Nirmāṇakāya forms is a facet of Total Realization, such realization means that one has gone beyond all limits and all forms. One has made manifest that state which always is, and was one's true condition from the beginning, and which itself can never be lost – though the *experience* of it is lost in the illusion of dualism. Total Realization means that one has realized one's identity with the ultimate ground of being, the Dharmakāya, the 'Body of Truth' or 'dimension of reality as it is'. It is this omnipresent void matrix, the Xí, or Base of every individual's being that manifests in the infinitely interpenetrating dance of the energies of the universe as the Sambhogakāya and Nirmāṇakāya forms of a realized being; or as the limited cage of karmic vision – the body, voice and mind – of a being trapped in dualism, who mistakes his or her own energy for a seemingly separate external world. (As explained in the section on *Dáñ*, *Rolba*, and *Zal*, on pp. 65–7.)

Total Realization means the definitive end of illusion, the end of suffering, the cessation of the vicious cycle of conditioned rebirths; it is the dawning of complete freedom, perfect wisdom, supreme unending bliss. In Total Realization death is overthrown, all duality transcended, and the capacity to spontaneously benefit all beings is perfectly manifested in a multiplicity of modes.

Of all the possible rebirths in any of the Six Realms birth in a human body is the most favourable for working towards Total Realization; and to be truly human, to fulfil truly one's humanity, such realization must be one's goal. Otherwise one lives one's life, as the Buddha pointed out, like a preoccupied child playing with toys in a house that is burning to the ground. For an ordinary human being death is real, and may come at any time, without warning. To waste one's precious human rebirth in trivial concerns is a tragedy. Only practice leads to one's own realization, and only through one's own realization can one ultimately help others, manifesting the capacities to be able to guide them to attain that same state themselves; any material assistance one can offer can only ever be provisional. To be able to help others one must therefore begin by helping oneself, however contradictory that may sound. Just as in counting to a million one must begin counting at the number one, so to benefit society one must begin by working on oneself. Each individual must truly take responsibility for him or herself, and this can only be done by working to increase one's awareness, to become more fully conscious, more the master of oneself.

Change on a small scale can bring about change on a wider scale; the influence of one being who is progressing towards realization can be powerful both at the level of subtle spiritual influence and in the concrete terms of influencing society. My own master Jyǎñqub Dórjé, for example, was not someone who was considered to be a master because he had been officially recognized as a reincarnation. Rather he was an ordinary person who had followed several great Zógqen masters, and who had put what they had taught him into practice. Through the power of his practice he had manifested great clarity, and so as a result of his qualities he had come to be regarded as a master. Disciples then began to gather around him. He didn't live in a monastery, but in an ordinary house, as I have already remarked in other stories, and his disciples, who included both monks and lay people, as they came to live around him, gradually built more houses as the years went by, until a village of practitioners had grown up around him. The kind of village that developed is known as a 'Gár', a term which has the sense of being the temporary or seasonal residence of nomads who may move on at any time, such as, for example, when all the grass in an area has been grazed.

With the passing of time all kinds of people, young and old, rich and poor, came to live together in Jyăṅqub Dórjé's Gár. There was a daily provision of free soup and simple fare for those who had no resources of their own, and this was paid for by those who had more than sufficient for their needs. Inspired by the master everyone offered what contributions they could to the needs of the whole community. Those practitioners who lacked private means were thus enabled to live, receive teachings, and practice at the Gár; but everyone who lived there worked every day participating in the hard physical labour of cultivating the fields, as well as collecting herbs and preparing medicines. In this way, as the influence of the master spread through this group of individuals drawn from all walks of life and all social strata, and as each individual's awareness developed, a kind of cooperative that was unknown at that time in Tibet spontaneously arose. The master never decreed that this was the way things should be; he encouraged the development of the awareness of his disciples, and out of their awareness evolved this response to their practical situation and everyday needs. The pattern of the Gár was quite different from the feudal system that still generally prevailed.

Many years later the Chinese began to make considerable inroads into Tibet, and finally reached the point of being in a position to be able to carry out what was called the 'Democratic Agrarian Reform' in the area of Jyăñqub Dórjé's Gár. Chinese officials and Tibetan functionaries from the Chinese offices were going everywhere visiting villages and monasteries to give them a thorough inspection with a view to reforming radically the structures of their institutions and their patterns of labour and ownership. I myself was at Jyăñqub Dórjé's Gár when a group of such officials arrived there, and can state that a visit by them was not at all like a pleasant social visit but involved a very thorough enquiry that would usually lead to very drastic and sweeping changes. But as the four Chinese officials and their Tibetan functionaries carried out their inspection they became more and more surprised by what they found. Since I can speak Chinese I was able to understand what they were saying to each other. They found it extremely strange that this master and the group of people who lived around him had already lived for many years as a perfectly functioning agricultural commune, completely in accordance with the Chinese socialist definition of such a thing. There was nothing to be changed; no reform needed to be carried out. Thus the Gár was allowed to continue exactly as it had done before, and even when Tibet was finally annexed by China, the Gár continued to function as a place of communal spiritual practice. While tragedy engulfed all the monasteries of Tibet as they collapsed or were destroyed, all that was changed of the Gár was its name. The practitioners who lived there renamed it 'Liberation Commune' which meant one thing to the Chinese who believed they had liberated Tibet, and another thing to those following the path of self-liberation!

Jyăñqub Dórjé continued to teach throughout all the tumultuous changes that overtook Tibet, and that he was able to do so was a direct result of the awareness of the practitioners of his Gár manifesting as the function of their practice in their daily lives. We walk, we work, we eat, and we sleep, and all of these activities must be permeated with our practice so that none of our time is wasted in our progress towards realization. Thus, although Jyǎṅqub Dórjé was continually active for the benefit of others, and worked every day at his practice of medicine, his own progress towards realization was in no way impaired. Despite his ordinary life-style he was a thoroughly extraordinary man.

When Jyǎṅqub Dórjé had arrived in the region where his Gár gradually grew up around him, he was already an old man. People would ask him how old he was, and he would always reply that he was seventy. He was still saying that he was seventy when I met him in 1955, which was sixty years after his arrival in that region. I myself asked him several times, out of curiosity how old he was, and he always told me that he was seventy. But the people of the area reckoned that he must at that time have been at least one hundred and thirty years old.

Now more than twenty years have passed since I left Tibet, and throughout those years I have had contact with my master in my dream practice. By this means I knew that he was still alive. Then, in 1980 I had news from three separate sources that my master and his daughter, who was also a practitioner of Zógqen, had died in unusual circumstances. When I myself returned to Tibet in 1981 for a visit, taking my wife and children, I heard from some of his disciples that both Jyǎṅqub Dórjé and his daughter, before they died, had asked to be left closed up in their rooms for seven days. Unfortunately, however, they had both been disturbed before the completion of that period of time. When the closed rooms were opened it was found that their bodies had shrunk to be about three feet in length. So it was clear that they had triumphantly brought their lives in a physical body to an end by manifesting one mode of realization of the Body of Light.

As a result of my coming to live in the West I

all over the world in response to
teach Zógqen. May the inspiration
d teachings of Jyăñqub Dórjé be a
ening for those who hear of them,
may be!
des the presentation here of the Base,
the Fruit of the Zógqen teachings. In
e teachings, words and intellectual
nly ever be signposts pointing to the
of reality beyond them. Yet the
linked conceptual structure of the
itself brilliant and beautiful, like a
crystal whose every facet flawlessly
fers to every other. But the only way
e heart of the crystal is to look into
en is not just something to be
Way of Light is there to be travelled.

As a bee seeks nectar
from all kinds of flowers,
seek teachings everywhere;
like a deer that finds
a quiet place to graze,
seek seclusion to digest
all you have gathered.
Like a madman,
beyond all limits,
go wherever you please;
and live like a lion,
completely free of all fear.

A tantra of Zógqen

Plates

Commentary

Plate 1   In this contemporary tañka, or painting traditionally done on cotton material so as to be easily rolled
up for carrying, Gárab Dórjé, the first master of Zógqen
to manifest on this planet in this time cycle (184 BC),
appears in a luminous tigle of visionary light above
Azòm Drùgba, one of the great Zógqen masters of the
late nineteenth and early twentieth centuries. Gárab
Dórjé is here shown in the form of a Mahāsiddha, a
realized tantric practitioner, though he is also sometimes
represented in a form similar to that used to depict the
historical buddha, Śākyamuni. Beside Gárab Dórjé, who
is seated on a deerskin, is a tantric gourd, used to
contain secret ritual objects, texts, etc. Azòm Drùgba is
shown wearing the ordinary clothes of a Tibetan layman,
with a fine formal silk robe over them, seated on his
teaching cushion, ready to give teaching. On the small
table in front of him are (l. to r.): a small ḍamaru; bell
and dórjé; a meloñ or mirror used as a symbol to explain
certain aspects of the teachings; and a skull cup offering
bowl.

Plates 2 and 3   No commentary; see captions.

Plate 4   Núben Sañgyás Yexes was a great accomplished
yogi, or Siddha, whose activities helped to ensure the
survival and continuation of the teachings established in
Tibet by Padmasambhava. During the period after
Padmasambhava had left Tibet in which the Buddhist
Dharma, after its initial spread, was suppressed for
political reasons, it was virtually impossible for a
community of monks to practise openly in the monas-

teries. The transmission and practice of the teachings was then carried forward by lay practitioners under the guidance of such masters as Núbqen Sañgyás Yexes, who lived and practised discreetly in lay communities in remote villages and mountain retreats far from the centres of political power. The teachings were thus preserved until the political climate once again became more favourable. Núbqen Sañgyás Yexes was expert in controlling negative influences, and is shown in this detail wielding his purba to drive away demons. A yogi flies in the air above his cave, and the syllable Hūṃ, symbol of the primordial state, manifests from a mountain.

Plate 5 In the teachings, energy as a general principle is regarded as feminine (receptive), while matter or substance is regarded as male (active). Thus the class of beings that manifest as, or dominate certain aspects of, energy are considered feminine, and are called 'Ḍākinī' in Sanskrit, or 'Kàdrò' (lit: 'space-dweller') in Tibetan. There are both worldly and non-worldly Ḍākinīs, and they are classed in five groups, like the five Dhyāni Buddhas, according to their type of activity. Non-worldly Ḍākinīs are Sambhogakāya manifestations like Siṃhamukha (p. 39) and Vajra Yogini: they are of the Buddha family, and are manifestations of the supreme activity of total realization. Then there are Ḍākinīs connected with the aspects of worldly activity of the Vajra, Ratna, Padma and Karma families, associated with the energy of the various aspects of wisdom. Some Ḍākinīs manifest as Guardians, like Ekajati (p. 96), some as human beings, and some as evil spirits. There are many kinds, and they can be either peaceful or wrathful, creative or destructive.

Gárab Dórjé, during his lifetime on Earth, taught the Ḍākinīs for many years before he taught human beings. He prophesied that, of the beings who would realize the Zógqen teachings, the majority would be female. This is perhaps because of the vast numbers of Ḍākinīs that exist. Hundreds of thousands of Ḍākinīs can have continuous contact with a master who has realized the Body of Light, whereas such contact is more difficult for ordinary human beings.

Padmasambhava also taught many Ḍākinīs for four years after his miraculous birth near the Dhanakosa lake, and he is considered to be always surrounded by a court of them. The Ḍākinīs have thus come to be in charge of many teachings which have been entrusted to their care either by Padmasambhava himself, or by his consort Yexes Cògyal. Ḍākinīs, and the class of beings associated with watery places known as 'Nāgas', guard a derma, or 'hidden treasure', until the time is ripe for its rediscovery and revelation by a 'Derdon' (Terton). Derdons are reincarnations of the principal disciples of Padmasambhava, and other masters, who have particular connection with the eighteen various kinds of hidden treasures Padmasambhava decided to conceal for future generations.

Padmasambhava lived in the ninth century A.D., and he prophesied that there would arise in the future three 'Grand', eight 'Great', twenty-one 'Powerful', 108 'Intermediate', and 1,000 'Intermediate' derdons of various kinds. A discoverer of texts is only one type of derdon, and needs visionary clarity not only to find the text, but also to interpret its meaning, as derma are often revealed in the language of the Ḍākinīs.

Through the ongoing process of the discovery of derma the teachings have been continually renewed and refined as they have been passed on, instead of becoming less clear, or even lost altogether, as might have happened if only an oral transmission had existed.

Plate 6 Mandāravā holds a vase of long life in her left hand. In her right hand she holds a 'Dàddăr', a ritual arrow, whose straight shaft represents the life force of the individual as an active principle of the primordial state. Attached to the arrow shaft are: a meloñ, or mirror, which here, since it reflects everything, represents the all-encompassing nature of the primordial state; and five coloured ribbons, whose fluttering represents the continual movement of the five elements which are carried on the prāṇa, or life force, and enable the development and continual regeneration of the physical body to occur. Above Mandāravā the Ḍākinīs of the five families bear offerings.

Plate 7 No commentary; see captions.

Plate 8 Vairocana was one of the first seven Buddhist

monks to be ordained in Tibet, receiving his vows from Śantarakṣita. He was later requested by Padmasambhava and the king of Tibet, Trisòñ Dézan, to go to Odiyana to seek teachings there to bring back to Tibet. He set out on the journey accompanied by another Tibetan master, and when they reached Tibet they spent a long time with Śrī Siṃha, a disciple of Mañjuśrimitra, Gárab Dórjé's principal disciple, who transmitted the Zógqen Semdé teachings to them. Vairocana's companion, satisfied with these teachings, then set out to return to Tibet, but died on the way. Vairocana remained in Odiyana for another two years to receive further teachings from Śrī Siṃha, and then returned to Tibet, where he was to give teachings to the King. Certain political factions at the court, however, sought to discredit Vairocana by claiming that the teachings he had brought back were false, and he was exiled to east Tibet for many years. In that part of east Tibet there was a local ruler who had a young son called Yúdrá Ñiñbo. When this boy met Vairocana he was at once able to understand all the teachings Vairocana gave him. He also manifested many Zógqen teachings from his own memory although he was too young ever to have studied them. Vairocana recognized him as the reincarnation of his companion on the journey to Odiyana, and he became Vairocana's principal disciple, later also becoming a disciple of Padmasambhava.

Vairocana ultimately regained favour with the King when Vimālamitra convinced Trisòñ Dézan that Vairocana's teachings were authentic, and Vairocana returned to the court, where together with Vimālamitra, Yexes Cògyal, and the King he was instrumental in spreading the teachings throughout Tibet.

Plates 9 and 10   No commentary; see captions.

Plate 11   The fifth Dalai Láma's personal temple is known as 'Zóñdag Lúkañ', and three walls of the murals it contains represent visions related to the Zógqen teachings. One wall illustrates a commentary by Lóñqenba on a Zógqen tantra called the 'Rigba Rañxar', interpreted according to the fifth Dalai Láma's own experience of practice, showing characteristic visions of the secret practice of Todgál that leads to the realization of the Body of Light, or Rainbow Body. Another wall shows the eight manifestations of Padmasambhava and the eighty-four principal Mahāsiddhas of the tantric tradition. The third wall illustrates positions and movements of Yantra Yoga, a specifically Tibetan form of yoga. There are Yantra Yoga movements found in the indigenous Bön traditions, as well as in the Buddhist Anuttaratantra.

These murals have never before been photographed because the temple is closed to the public by the authorities. The author managed to photograph them whilst revisiting Tibet in 1981, his first opportunity to visit his native land for more than twenty years.

Plates 12 and 13 The Sanskrit 'Yantra' is 'Trùlkòr' in Tibetan, while the Sanskrit 'Yoga' becomes the Tibetan 'Náljyòr'. 'Trùlkòr' means 'Magic Wheel', with an implied meaning of 'machine', or 'engine'. 'Náljyòr' is composed of the noun 'nálma', and the verb 'jyòrba'. 'Nálma' means 'the natural, unaltered state' of anything, and 'jyòrba' means 'to possess'. Thus, if we put the terms 'Trùlkòr' and 'Náljyòr' together, we can see that Yantra Yoga is a method for the individual to arrive at his or her natural state or condition by way of using the human body like a machine that, once set in motion, produces a specific effect. The practical difference between Yantra Yoga and the Indian Hatha Yoga which is at present more widely known in the West is that Yantra works with a system of bodily movements linked to breathing, rather than with fixed positions, which are the basis of Hatha Yoga. The realizations aimed at are also fundamentally different in the two systems.

Plates 14-27 No commentary; see captions.

1 Gárab Dórjé, the first Zógqen master on this planet in this time cycle, and below him Azòm Drùgba, one of the great Tibetan Zógqen masters of the late nineteenth and early twentieth centuries. (Tañka by Nigel Wellings; collection Bill Palmer, photo: Susan Bagley.)

2 Tañka showing the ninth century A.D. master Padmasambhava as a Mahāpaṇḍita,
with his two principal female disciples Yeshes Cògyal and Mandāravā, surrounded by
scenes depicting masters involved in the early spread of the Buddhist Dharma in Tibet.
There would usually be a series of two or three such tañkas representing the life of
Padmasambhava. Enlarged details of this tañka, with explanation, will be found on the
following pages. (Tañka by an unknown artist; collection John Shane; photo: Susan
Bagley.)

3 This detail from the tañka on the facing page shows Padmasambhava flanked by his two principal consorts. He holds a Dórjé (Tibetan), or Vajra (Sanskrit), in his right hand, and a skull cup offering bowl in his left. Yexes Còyal, on his right, holds the great master's ritual trident or Katvamga (Sanskrit). (Photo: Susan Bagley.)

4 This tañka detail shows Núbqen Sañgyás Yexes who was a disciple of both Padmasambhava and Yexes Còyal. He realized the practice of Yamāntaka, one of the eight Herukas, or Déxèg Gagyád, whose practices Padmasambhava transmitted to his principal disciples. Yamantaka is thus shown appearing above Núbqen Sañgyás Yexes, just as in other details of the tañka the other Herukas are shown above the masters most associated with their practices. As a sign of his realization Núbqen Sañgyás Yexes was able to pierce solid rock with his purba, or ritual dagger, shown in his right hand. (Photo: Susan Bagley.)

5 This detail from the tañka in plate 2 shows Yexes Cògyal (Yeshe Tsogyal), one of Padmasambhava's chief disciples and tantric consorts, giving two 'Derma' (terma) or 'hidden treasures', one a reliquary, the other a text, to three Dākinīs who kneel respectfully before her. Two of the Dākinīs wear magic shawls of human skin. A being of the Nāga class rises from his watery domain to receive treasures into his safe keeping (below right). Two Derma can be seen already concealed in the rocks above Yexes Cògyal. (Photo: Susan Bagley.)

6. Detail of the tañka of the life of Padmasambhava showing his great Indian-born disciple and consort Mandāravā, manifesting as a dancing Ḍākinī in a human body. (Photo: Susan Bagley.)

7 This tañka detail shows one of Padmasambhava's principal female disciples (probably Kālasiddhi) manifesting in a form similar to that of White Tārā, to give teachings to disciples assembled before her. One disciple bears a pile of texts bound in silk. Above Kālasiddhi one of the eight Herukas, or Déxèg Gagyád, manifests. (Photo: Susan Bagley.)

8 This tañka detail shows the Vairocana (top left), the great translator contemporary
of Padmasambhava, above whom appears the Heruka Dobdán Nagbo in union with his
consort. Below right, Yúdrá Ñìñbo, Vairocana's principal disciple is seated in meditation,
surrounded by rays of rainbow light and luminous tigle, manifestations of his realized
energy. Samantabadra in union with his consort appears in the uppermost tigle, symbol
of the Dharmakāya. To the left of Yúdrá Ñìñbo is the figure of Bañ Mipam Gònbo, who
was a disciple of Yúdrá Ñìñbo, and a famous disciple of Vairocana. (Photo: Susan
Bagley.)

9 Detail of tañka showing one of the foremost disciples of Vairocana, Palgi Yexes, who was also the chief disciple of Jñanakumara, a translator colleague of Vairocana. Palgi Yexes gained control of the Mamo class of Guardians, and is shown here with them appearing to him. Above him another of the eight Herukas manifests in union with his consort. (Photo: Susan Bagley.)

10 Detail of the tañka of the life of Padmasambhava and early spread of the Buddhist Dharma in Tibet, showing the great master holding a Vajra and offering a skull cup of nectar to a Heruka who manifests to him surrounded by flames. (Photo: Susan Bagley.)

11 The great fifth Dalai Láma, Gyálqòg Nába (1617–82), is represented in this taṅka. He was the first Dalai Láma to hold temporal power over all Tibet as well as spiritual authority as the head of the Gelugba school. He was a great Zógqen practitioner, outwardly manifesting conduct perfectly in accordance with his various responsibilities. He began the building of the great Potala palace, just outside Lhasa below and behind which, on an island at the centre of a lake, he began building a small secret temple for his personal use, called Zóṅdag Lúkaṅ, whose interior walls were covered with murals. (Taṅka by unknown Tibetan artist; Photo: Brian Beresford.)

12 and 13 Two details from the murals in the fifth Dalai Láma's secret temple, 'Zóñdag Lúkân', showing yogis practising Yantra Yoga. (Photos: Namkhai Norbu.)

14 and 15 These two details from the murals in the fifth Dalai Láma's secret temple show yogis in various practice positions, with the Tibetan letter 'Ah', a symbol of the primordial state of the mind, much used as an object of fixation, appearing in 'tigle' spheres of rainbow light. Different positions of the body, combined with specific breathing patterns, influence the flow of the individual's subtle energy, and thus the individual's state of mind. (Photos: Namkhai Norbu.)

16 This detail from the Todgál mural in the fifth Dalai Láma's secret temple shows yogis practising in a mountain landscape, surrounded by various visionary apparitions manifesting as the function of their practice's progress. At the top left, the Buddha and five Ḍākinīs manifest in spheres of rainbow light, or 'tigle', below which a yogi is shown engaged in the practice of developing inner fire, or heat, as a means to realizing the union of sensation and voidness. Flames rise above his head from the central of his three principal channels, where a Tibetan letter 'Ah' manifests in a stream of five coloured light. (Photo: Namkhai Norbu.)

17 This enlargement of the previous detail from the Todgál mural shows more clearly, in two of the yogi's bodies, the position of the three principal channels of subtle energy. The yogi who is seen from behind is practising to integrate his energy with the element water. He is gazing at the moving water of a waterfall, while fixing his attention on its sound. The letter 'Ah' visualized at the centre of his body, superimposed over his central channel, is echoed by the external manifestation of a large watery letter 'Ah' to his right. (Photo: Namkhai Norbu.)

18 Here the author, Namkhai Norbu Rinpoche, at a retreat he led in California, USA in 1981, is seated in a Lóñdé position similar to the position in which Milarasba is usually shown, but with the meditation belt in place as an aid to maintaining the posture.

19 Another Lóñdé position, with both knees raised, and both thumbs pressing on the 'Wave of Bliss' in each side of the neck. (Photos: Tsultrim Allione.)

20 Another of the positions of the Lóñdé. In all the positions the mouth is kept open, with the tongue neither touching the roof nor the floor. The eyes, considered the 'Gates of Wisdom', are also kept open and unblinking.

21 The meditation stick presses on a pressure point in the armpit, and also serves to keep the spine absolutely straight. Stick and belt are provisional aids to help the practitioner maintain the positions of the Lóñdé, whose purpose is to control the flow of prāṇa, or subtle energy, so that it remains in the central channel.

22 When the prāṇa is in the central channel, the mind is in contemplation. Prāṇa normally circulates in either the solar or lunar channel, and changes from one to the other twice in every 24 hours. The position used in the morning is therefore the mirror image of that used in the afternoon. At the time when the prāṇa is normally in the channel on the right side of the body, the left leg is raised, and vice versa. The prāṇic flow in the body of a woman is the mirror image of that in a man, and so women practise, at any given time of day, the mirror image of whatever position a man would practise at that same moment.

23 The Lóñdé positions work with the union of sensation of emptiness, through which visionary clarity is developed to an ultimate degree. Although the Lóñdé practices do not require any intellectual understanding on the part of the practitioner, but work to bring one directly into the experience of the primordial state, transmission from a master is essential. Without it they will not function. The descriptions of these positions are not complete instructions for practice. (Photos: Tsultrim Allione.)

24 A Tibetan monk in India puts the finishing touches to a statue of the great Tibetan yogi poet Milarasba (Milarepa). Statues depicting Milarasba in this position are traditional, and are generally titled 'Milarasba listening to the sound of the Universe', as if his hand was raised to his ear to help him to hear. But, as can be seen by comparison with the preceding plates, he is in fact practising a yogic position similar to the positions of the Lóndé. (Photo: Brian Beresford.)

25 Detail of taňka showing Milarasba's principal disciple kneeling to stare into a yak's horn lying on the ground within which Milarasba is sheltering from a hailstorm (see story p. 123). (Photo: Brian Beresford.)

26 His Holiness Tenzin Gyatso, the fourteenth Dalai Láma, at a Zógqen teaching given by him in London in 1984, holding a crystal with a peacock feather attached above it. These were used as ritual implements in the initiation he gave, the crystal representing the practices of the Tregqod, and the peacock feather representing Todgál. (Photo: Brian Beresford.)

27 Detail from the Todgál mural in the fifth Dalai Láma's secret temple showing a yogi holding a crystal which reflects the sun's rays. Crystals are much used in the Zógqen teachings as a symbol of the way in which the individual's own mind projects what appears to the individual as a seemingly 'external' reality. (Photo: Namkhai Norbu.)

28 Namkhai Norbu Rinpoche practising during a Spring 1984 retreat in the cave at Maratika in Nepal in which, many years before, Padmasambhava himself received transmission of and realized the practice of Amitāyus, the Buddha of Long Life (see p. 89). (Photo: Dzogchen Community.)

Key to the Groups of Three in the Zógqen teachings

NB: A linear diagram cannot truly represent the complex inter-relationships of the various aspects of the teachings, which would be better represented by a three dimensional crystalline structure, each of whose points connected with every other. But, since a book is a linear presentation because of the very nature of language and how it is written, the teaching, when written in a book, has to be presented in a linear sequence. So this diagram is only intended as a provisional key to be of use towards opening up a more subtle vision of the many correspondences in the crystal of the teachings, and as an aid to following the argument of the book.

The Primordial State, or 1 BASE of every individual (Xi)	which comprises:	ESSENCE. (which is void) NATURE (Yet manifestation continues to occur) ENERGY (which manifests in three characteristic ways as:			
			DÁN	These, as is explained by the metaphors of the crystal and its rays, the crystal ball, and the mirror and its reflections, are one's own energy. Yet a being in Samsara mistakes them for external phenomena, and sees them as his karmic vision, comprising respectively:	MIND
			ROLBA		VOICE (or respiratory energy)
			ZAL		BODY

MIND
VOICE
BODY

The true view is to observe the condition of one's own

DAVA — View, or vision of what is, and what one is

The 2 PATH: (Lam)

GÓMBA — Actual practices, presented in the Three Series: (see separate diagram)

SEMDÉ — The Series of Mind.
LÓNDÉ — The Series of Space.
MANÑAGDÉ — The Essential Series.

There are practices that work with each of the aspects of the individual, Body, Voice, and Mind.

JYODBA — How one lives in the light of the View and the practice, carrying contemplation into every action of the 24 hours of one's daily life, governing one's attitude with awareness

There are *principal* and *secondary* practices.

PRINCIPLE PRACTICES: are the practice of contemplation, of Zógchen itself, and meditation practices leading one to be able to enter contemplation. The practices of TREGQOD help one to be able to continue in contemplation, while the practices of TODGÁL rapidly enable one to develop the state of contemplation, through vision, to its ultimate conclusion, in the realization of the Body of Light.

SECONDARY PRACTICES: are any practice that may be used together with contemplation, to develop a particular capacity, or to overcome a particular obstacle. (Yantra Yoga, recitation of mantras, ritual, and so on.)

Realization, or The 3 FRUIT: (Dràsbu)

THE GREAT TRANSFER
THE BODY OF LIGHT
} TOTAL REALIZATION

The Three 'Bodies'
DHARMAKÁYA
SAMBHOGAKÁYA
NIRMÁNAKÁYA

Which are three qualities of one's own being, when one realizes, or makes real The BASE, the state that is one's own condition from the very beginning

The Mirror

Advice on presence and awareness

This short text by Namkhai Norbu Rinpoche was originally written in Tibetan. It was then translated into Italian by Adriano Clemente and into English by John Shane, and was published as a small pamphlet on the occasion of the first International Conference on Tibetan Medicine, held in Venice and Arcidosso, Italy, 1983. It is included here as a precise and detailed instruction on the most essential aspect of Zógqen practice.

I pay homage to my Master!

A practitioner of *rDzogs-chen* must have precise presence and awareness. Until one really and truly knows one's own mind and can govern it with awareness, even if very many explanations of reality are given, they remain nothing more than ink on paper or matters for debate among intellectuals, without the possibility of the birth of any understanding of the real meaning.

In the *Kun-byed rgyal-po*,[1] a *tantra* of *rDzogs-chen*, it is said that: 'The Mind is that which creates both *Samsāra* and *Nirvāna*, so one needs to know this King which creates everything!'

We say we transmigrate in the impure and illusory vision of *Samsāra*, but in reality, it's just our mind that is transmigrating.

And then again, as far as pure Enlightenment is concerned, it's only our own mind, purified, that realizes it.

Our mind is the basis of everything, and from our mind everything arises, *Samsāra* and *Nirvāna*, ordinary sentient beings and Enlightened Ones.

Consider the way beings transmigrate in the impure vision of *Samsāra*: even though the Essence of the Mind, the true nature of our mind, is totally pure right from the beginning, nevertheless, because pure mind is temporarily obscured by the impurity of ignorance, there is no self-recognition of our own State. Through this lack of self-recognition arise illusory thoughts and actions created by the passions. Thus various negative karmic causes are accumulated and since their maturation as effects is inevitable, one suffers bitterly, transmigrating in the six states of existence.[2] Thus, not recognizing one's own State is the cause of transmigration, and through this cause one becomes the slave of illusions and distractions. Conditioned by the mind, one becomes strongly habituated to illusory actions.

And then it's the same as far as pure Enlightenment is concerned; beyond one's own mind there is no dazzling light to come shining in from outside to wake one up. If one recognizes one's own intrinsic State as pure from the beginning and only temporarily obscured by impurities, and if one maintains the presence of this recognition without becoming distracted, then all the impurities dissolve. This is the essence of the Path.

Then the inherent quality of the great original purity of the Primordial State manifests, and one recognizes it and becomes the master of it as a lived experience.

This experience of the real knowledge of the authentic original condition, or the true awareness of the State, is what is called *Nirvāna*. So Enlightenment is nothing other than one's own mind in its purified condition.

For this reason Padma Sambhava[3] said: 'The mind is the creator of *Samsāra* and of *Nirvāna*. Outside the mind there exists neither *Samsāra* nor *Nirvāna*.'

Having thus established that the basis of *Samsāra* and *Nirvāna* is the mind, it follows that all that seems concrete in the world, and all the seeming solidity of beings themselves, is nothing but an illusory vision of one's own mind. Just as a person who has a 'bile' disease sees a shell as being yellow even if one can see objectively that that is not its true colour, so in just the same way, as a result of the particular karmic causes of sentient beings, the various illusory visions manifest.

Thus, if one were to meet a being of each of the six states of existence on the bank of the same river, they would not see that river in the same way, since they each would have different karmic causes. The beings of the hot hells would see the river as fire; those of the cold hells would see it as ice; beings of the hungry ghost realm would see the river as blood and pus; aquatic animals would see it as an environment to live in; human beings would see the river as water to drink; while the demi-gods would see it as weapons, and the gods as nectar.

This shows that in reality nothing exists as concrete and objective. Therefore, understanding that the root of *Samsāra* is truly the mind, one should set out to pull up the root. Recognizing that the mind itself is the essence of Enlightenment one attains liberation.

Thus, being aware that the basis of *Samsāra* and *Nirvāna* is only the mind, one takes the decision to practise. At this point, with mindfulness and determination, it is necessary to maintain a continuous present awareness without becoming distracted.

If, for example, one wants to stop a river from flowing, one must block it at its source, in such a way that its flow is definitively interrupted; whatever other point you may choose to block it at, you will not obtain the same result. Similarly, if we want to cut the root of *Samsāra*, we must cut the root of the mind that has created it; otherwise there would be no way of becoming free of *Samsāra*. If we want all the suffering and hindrances arising from our negative actions to dissolve, we must cut the root of the mind which produced them.

If we don't do this, even if we carry out virtuous actions with our body and voice, there will be no result beyond a momentary fleeting benefit. Besides, never having cut the root of negative actions, they can once again be newly accumulated, in just the same way that if one only lops off a few leaves and branches from a tree instead of cutting its main root, far from the tree shrivelling up, it will without doubt grow once again.

If the mind, the King which creates everything, is not left in its natural condition, even if one practises the tantric methods of the 'Developing' and 'Perfecting' stages,[4] and recites many mantras, one is not on the path to total liberation. If one wants to conquer a country, one must subjugate the King or the Lord of that country; just to subjugate a part of the population or some functionary won't bring about the fulfilment of one's aim.

If one does not maintain a continuous presence, and lets oneself be dominated by distractions, one will never liberate oneself from endless *Samsāra*. On the other hand, if one doesn't allow oneself to be dominated by neglectfulness and illusions, but has self-control, knowing how to continue in the true State with present awareness, then one unites in oneself the essence of all the Teachings, the root of all the Paths.

Because all the various factors of dualistic vision, such as *Samsāra* and *Nirvāna*, happiness and suffering, good and bad, etc., arise from the mind, we can conclude that the mind is their fundamental basis. This is why non-distraction is the root of the Paths and the fundamental principle of the practice.

It was by following this supreme path of continuous presence that all the Buddhas of the past became enlightened, by following this same path the Buddhas of the future will become enlightened, and the Buddhas of the present, following this right path, are enlightened. Without following this Path, it is not possible to attain enlightenment.

Therefore, because the continuation in the presence of the true State is the essence of all the Paths, the root of all meditations, the conclusion of all spiritual practices, the juice of all esoteric methods, the heart of all ultimate teachings, it is necessary to seek to maintain a continuous presence without becoming distracted.

What this means is: don't follow the past, don't anticipate the future, and don't follow illusory thoughts that arise in the present; but turning within oneself, one should observe one's own true condition and maintain the awareness of it just as it is, beyond conceptual limitations of the 'three times'.

One must remain in the uncorrected condition of one's own natural state, free from the impurity of judgments between 'being and non-being', 'having and not-having', 'good and bad', and so on.

The original condition of the Great Perfection is truly beyond the limited conceptions of the 'three times'; but those who are just beginning the practice, at any rate, do not yet have this awareness and find it difficult to experience the recognition of their own State; it is therefore very important not to allow oneself to be distracted by the thoughts of the 'three times'.

If, in order not to become distracted, one tries to eliminate all one's thoughts, becoming fixated on the search for a state of calm or a sensation of pleasure, it is necessary to remember that this is an error, in that the very 'fixation' one is engaged in is, in itself, nothing but another thought.

One should relax the mind, maintaining only the awakened presence of one's own State, without allowing oneself to be dominated by any thought whatsoever. When one is truly relaxed, the mind finds itself in its natural condition.

If out of this natural condition thoughts arise, whether good or bad, rather than trying to judge whether one is in the calm state or in the wave of thoughts, one should just acknowledge all thoughts with the awakened presence of the State itself.

When thoughts are given just this bare attention of simple acknowledgment, they relax into their own true condition, and as long as this awareness of their relaxedness lasts one should not forget to keep the mind present. If one becomes distracted and does not simply acknowledge the thoughts, then it is necessary to give more attention to making one's awareness truly present.

If one finds that thoughts arise about finding oneself in a state of calm, without abandoning simple presence of mind, one should continue by observing the state of movement of the thought itself.

In the same way, if no thoughts arise, one should continue with the presence of the simple acknowledgment that just gives bare attention to the state of calm. This means maintaining the presence of this natural state, without attempting to fix it within any conceptual framework or hoping for it to manifest in any particular form, colour, or light, but just relaxing into it, in a condition undisturbed by the characteristics of the ramifications of thought.

Even if those who begin to practise this find it difficult to continue in this state for more than an instant, there is no need to worry about it. Without wishing for the state to continue for a long time and without fearing the lack of it altogether, all that is necessary is to maintain pure presence of mind, without falling into the dualistic situation of there being an observing subject perceiving an observed object.

If the mind, even though one maintains simple presence, does not remain in this calm state, but always tends to follow waves of thoughts about the past or future, or becomes distracted by the aggregates of the senses such as sight, hearing, etc., then one should try to understand that the wave of thought itself is as insubstantial as the wind. If one tries to catch the wind, one does not succeed; similarly if one tries to block the wave of thought, it cannot be cut off. So for this reason one should not try to block thought, much less try to renounce it as something considered negative.

In reality, the calm state is the essential condition of mind, while the wave of thought is the mind's natural clarity in function; just as there is no distinction whatever between the sun and its rays, or a stream and its ripples, so there is no distinction between the mind and thought. If one considers the calm state as something positive to be attained, and the wave of thought as something negative to be abandoned, and one remains thus caught up in the duality of accepting and rejecting, there is no way of overcoming the ordinary state of mind.

Therefore the essential principle is to acknowledge with bare attention, without letting oneself become distracted, whatever thought arises, be it good or bad, important or less important, and to continue to maintain presence in the state of the moving wave of thought itself.

When a thought arises and one does not succeed in remaining calm with this presence, since other such thoughts may follow, it is necessary to be skilful in acknowledging it with non-distraction. 'Acknowledging' does not mean seeing it with one's eyes, or forming a concept about it. Rather it means giving bare attention, without distraction to whatever thought of the 'three times', or whatever perception of the senses may arise, and thus being fully conscious of this 'wave' while continuing in the presence of the pure awareness. It absolutely does not mean modifying the mind in some way, such as by trying to imprison thought or to block its flow.

It is difficult for this acknowledgment with bare attention, without distraction, to last for a long time for someone who is beginning this practice, as a result of strong mental habits of distraction acquired through transmigration in the course of unlimited time. If we only take into consideration this present lifetime, from the moment of our birth right up until the present we have done nothing other than live distractedly, and there has never been an opportunity to train in the presence of awareness and non-distraction. For this reason, until we become no longer capable of entering into distraction, if, through lack of attention, we find ourselves becoming dominated by neglectfulness and forgetfulness, we must try by every means to become aware of what is happening through relying on the presence of mind.

There is no 'meditation' that you can find beyond this continuing in one's own true condition with the presence of the calm state, or with the moving wave of thought. Beyond recognition with bare attention and continuing in one's own State, there is nothing to seek that is either very good or very clear.

If one hopes that something will manifest from outside oneself, instead of continuing in the presence of one's own State, this is like the saying that tells about an evil spirit coming to the Eastern gate, and the ransom to buy him off being sent to the Western gate. In such a case, even if one believes one is meditating perfectly, in reality, it's just a way of tiring oneself out for nothing. So continuing in the State which one finds within oneself is really the most important thing.

If one neglects that which one has within oneself and instead seeks something else, one becomes like the beggar who had a precious stone for a pillow, but not knowing it for what it was, had to go to such great pains to beg for alms for a living.

Therefore, maintaining the presence of one's own State and observing the wave of thought, without judging whether this presence is more or less clear, and without thinking of the calm state and the wave of thought in terms of the acceptance of the one and the rejection of the other, absolutely not conditioned by wanting to change anything whatsoever, one continues without becoming distracted, and without forgetting to keep one's awareness present; governing oneself in this way one gathers the essence of the practice.

Some people are disturbed when they hear noises made by other people walking, talking and so on, and they become irritated by this, or else, becoming distracted by things external to themselves, they give birth to many illusions. This is the mistaken path known as 'the dangerous passageway in which external vision appears to one as an enemy'. What this means is that, even though one knows how to continue in the knowledge of the condition of both the state of calm and the wave of thought, one has not yet succeeded in integrating this state with one's external vision.

If this should be the case, while still always maintaining present awareness, if one sees something, one should not be distracted, but, without judging what one sees as pleasant, one should relax and continue in the presence.

If a thought arises judging experience as pleasant and unpleasant, one should just acknowledge it with bare attention and continue in present awareness without forgetting it.

If one finds oneself in an annoying circumstance, such as surrounded by a terrible row, one should just acknowledge this disagreeable circumstance and continue in present awareness, without forgetting it.

If one does not know how to integrate the presence of awareness with all one's daily actions, such as eating, walking, sleeping, sitting, and so on, then it is not possible to make the state of contemplation last beyond the limited duration of a session of sitting meditation. If this is so, not having been able to establish true present awareness, one creates a separation between one's sessions of sitting practice and one's daily life. So it is very important to continue in present awareness without distraction, integrating it with all the actions of one's daily life. The Buddha, in the *Prajñāpāramitā Sūtra*[5] said: 'Subhuti, in what way does a *Bodhisattva-Mahāsattva*, being aware that he has a body, practise perfect conduct? Subhuti, a *Bodhissattva-Mahāsattva*, when walking, is fully mindful that he is walking; when he stands up is fully mindful of standing up; when sitting is fully mindful of sitting; when sleeping is fully mindful of sleeping; and if his body is well or ill, he is fully mindful of either condition!' That's just how it is!

To understand how one can integrate present awareness with all the activities of one's daily life, let's take the example of walking. There's no need to jump up immediately and walk in a distracted and agitated way, marching up and down and breaking everything one finds in front of one, as soon as the idea of walking arises. Rather, as one gets up, one can do so remembering 'now I am getting up, and while walking I do not want to become distracted'.

In this way, without becoming distracted, step by step, one should govern oneself with the presence of awareness. In the same way, if one remains seated, one should not forget this awareness, and whether one is eating a tasty morsel, or having a drop to drink, or saying a couple of words, whatever action one undertakes, whether it is of greater or lesser importance, one should continue with present awareness of everything without becoming distracted.

Since we are so strongly habituated to distraction it is difficult to give birth to this presence of awareness, and this is especially true for those who are just beginning to practise. But whenever there's any new kind of work to be done, the first thing one has to do is to learn it. And even if at the first few attempts one is not very practised, with experience, little by little the work becomes easy. In the same way, in learning contemplation, at the beginning one needs commitment and a definite concern not to become distracted, following that one must maintain present awareness as much as possible, and finally, if one becomes distracted, one must notice it.

If one perseveres in one's commitment to maintaining present awareness, it is possible to arrive at a point where one no longer ever becomes distracted. In general, in *rDzogs-chen*, the Teaching of spontaneous self-perfection, one speaks of the self-liberation of the way of seeing, of the way of meditating, of the way of behaving, and of the fruit,[6] but this self-liberation must arise through the presence of awareness.

In particular, the self-liberation of the way of behaving absolutely cannot arise if it is not based on the presence of awareness. So, if one does not succeed in making the self-liberation of one's way of behaving precise, one cannot overcome the distinction between sessions of sitting meditation and one's daily life.

When we speak of the self-liberation of one's way of behaving as the fundamental principle of all the *tantra*, the *āgama*, and the *upadeśa*[7] of *rDzogs-chen*, this pleases the young people of today a great deal. But some of them do not know that the real basis of self-liberation is the presence of awareness, and many of them, even if they understand this a little in theory, and know how to speak of it, nevertheless, just the same have the defect of not applying it. If a sick person knows perfectly well the properties and functions of a medicine and is also expert in giving explanations about it, but doesn't ever take the medicine, he or she can never get well. In the same way, throughout limitless time we have been suffering from the serious illness of being subject to the dualistic condition, and the only remedy for this illness is real knowledge of the state of self-liberation without falling into limitations.

When one is in contemplation, in the continuation of the awareness of the true State, then it is not necessary to consider one's way of behaving as important, but, on the other hand, for someone who is beginning to practise, there is no way of entering into practice other than by alternating sessions of sitting meditation with one's daily life. This is because we have such strong attachment, based on logical thinking, on regarding the objects of our senses as being concrete, and, even more so, based on our material body made of flesh and blood.

148

When we meditate on the 'absence of self-nature', examining mentally our head and the limbs of our body, eliminating them one by one as 'without self', we can finally arrive at establishing that there is no 'self' or 'I'.

But this 'absence of self-nature' remains nothing but a piece of knowledge arrived at through intellectual analysis, and there is as yet no real knowledge of this 'absence of self-nature'. Because, while we are cosily talking about this 'absence of self-nature', if it should happen that we get a thorn in our foot, there's no doubt that we'll right away be yelping 'ow! ow! ow!' This shows that we are still subject to the dualistic condition and that the 'absence of self-nature' so loudly proclaimed with our mouth has not become a real lived state for us. For this reason it is indispensable to regard as extremely important the presence of awareness which is the basis of self-liberation in one's daily conduct.

Since there have been different ways of regarding conduct as important, there have arisen various forms of rules established according to the external conditions prevailing at the time, such as religious rules and judicial laws. There is, however, a great deal of difference between observing rules through compulsion and observing them through awareness. Since, in general, everyone is conditioned by *karma*, by the passions, and by dualism, there are very few people who observe rules and laws through awareness. For this reason, even if they don't want to do so, human beings have had obligatorily to remain subject to the power of various kinds of rules and laws.

We are already conditioned by *karma*, by the passions, and by dualism. If one then adds limitations derived from having compulsorily to follow rules and laws, our burden becomes even heavier, and without doubt we get even further from the correct 'way of seeing' and from the right 'way of behaving'.

If one understands the term 'self-liberating' as meaning that one can just do whatever one wants, this is not correct; this is absolutely not what the principle of self-liberation means, and to believe such a mistaken view would show that one has not truly understood what awareness means.

But then again we should not consider the principle of laws and rules as being just the same as the principle of awareness. Laws and rules are in fact established on the basis of circumstances of time and place, and work by conditioning the individual with factors outside him or herself. Awareness, on the other hand, arises from a state of knowledge which the individual him or herself possesses. Because of this, laws and rules sometimes correspond to the inherent awareness of the individual, and sometimes do not. However, if one has awareness, it is possible to overcome the situation of being bound by compulsion to follow rules and laws. Not only is this so, but an individual who has awareness and keeps it stably present is also capable of living in peace under all the rules and laws there are in the world, without being in any way conditioned by them.

Many Masters have said: 'Urge on the horse of awareness with the whip of presence!' And, in fact, if awareness is not quickened by presence it cannot function.

Let's examine an example of awareness: suppose that in front of a person in a normal condition there is a cup full of poison, and that person is aware of what it is. Adult and balanced persons, knowing the poison for what it is and aware of the consequences of taking it, do not need much clarification about it. But they have to warn those who don't know about the poison being there, by saying something like: 'In this cup there is some poison, and it's deadly if swallowed!' Thus, by creating awareness in others, the danger can be avoided. This is what we mean by awareness.

But there are cases of persons who, although they know the danger of the poison, don't give any importance to it, or still have doubts as to whether it really is a dangerous poison, or who really lack all awareness, and with these people it is simply not sufficient to just say: 'This is poison'. For them one has to say: 'It is forbidden to drink this substance, on pain of punishment by the law'. And through this kind of threat the law protects the lives of these individuals. This is the principle on which laws are based, and even if it is very different from the principle of awareness, it is nevertheless indispensable as a means to save the lives of those who are unconscious and without awareness.

Now we can continue the metaphor of the poison to show what we mean by presence. If the person who has a cup of poison in front of them, even though they are aware and know very well what the consequences of taking the poison would be, does not have a continuous presence of attention to the fact that the cup contains poison, it may happen that they become distracted and swallow some of it. So if awareness is not continually accompanied by presence it is difficult for there to be the right results. This is what we mean by presence.

In the *Mahāyāna*, the principle to which maximum importance is given, and the essence itself of the *Mahāyāna* doctrine, is the union of voidness and compassion. But, in truth, if one does not have awareness inseparably linked to presence, there absolutely cannot arise a really genuine compassion. As long as one does not have the real experience of being moved by compassion for others, it is useless to pretend that one is so very full of compassion. There is a Tibetan proverb about this which says: 'Even if you've got eyes to see other people, you need a mirror to see yourself!' As this proverb implies, if one really wants a genuine compassion for others to arise in oneself, it is necessary to observe one's own defects, be aware of them, and mentally put yourself in other people's places to really discover what those persons' actual conditions might be. The only way to succeed in this is to have the presence of awareness.

Otherwise, even if one pretends to have great compassion, a situation will sooner or later arise which shows that compassion has never really been born in us at all.

Until a pure compassion does arise, there is no way to overcome one's limits and barriers. And it happens that many practitioners, as they progress in the practice, just end up thinking of themselves as being a 'divinity' and thinking of everyone else as being 'evil spirits'. Thus they are doing nothing other than increasing their own limits, developing attachment towards themselves, and hatred towards others. Or, even if they talk a great deal about *Mahāmudrā*[8] and *rDzogs-chen*, all they are really doing is becoming more expert and refined in the ways of behaving of the eight worldly *dharma*.[9] This is a sure sign that a true compassion has not arisen in us, and the root of the matter is that there has never really arisen the presence of awareness.

So, without chattering about it, or getting caught up in trying to hide behind an elegant facade, one should try really and truly to cause the presence of awareness actually to arise in oneself, and then carry it into practice. This is the most important point of the practice of *rDzogs-chen*.

This book is dedicated by the practitioner of *rDzogs-chen*, Namkhai Norbu, to his disciples of the *rDzogs-chen* Community.

Into the lion's mouth!

Appendix 2

Biographical sketch of the author

This short biography was originally published in the second edition in Tibetan of the author's *Necklace of Gzi: A Cultural History of Tibet*, published by the Private Office of H.H. The Dalai Lama. It was translated into English by John Reynolds to be included in the author's booklet 'Dzogchen and Zen', published by Zhang Zung Editions, Oakland, California, 1984. It is included here as a more complete biography than Rinpoche's anecdotal account of his early life in the first chapter of this book. Since this biography will be of interest primarily to Tibetologists, we have left the Tibetan names and terms in the transcription system in which the material was originally published.

Nam mkha'i Norbu Rinpoche, was born in the village of dGe'ug, in the lCong ra district of sDe dge in East Tibet on the eighth day of the tenth month of the Earth-Tiger year (1938). His father was sGrol ma Tshe ring, member of a noble family and sometime official with the government of sDe dge, and his mother was Ye shes Chos sgron.

When he was two years old, dPal yul Karma Yang srid Rinpoche[1] and Zhe chen Rab byams Rinpoche,[2] both recognized him as the reincarnation of A'dzom 'Brug pa.[3] A'dzom 'Brug pa was one of the great rDzogs chen Masters of the early part of this century. He was the disciple of the first mKhyen brtse Rinpoche, 'Jam dbyangs mKhyen brtse dBang po (1829–92), and also the disciple of dPal sprul Rinpoche.[4] Both of these illustrious teachers were leaders of the *Ris med* or non-sectarian movement in nineteenth-century eastern Tibet. On some thirty-seven occasions, A'dzom

'Brug pa received transmissions from his principal master, 'Jam dbyangs mKhyen brtse, and from dPal sprul Rinpoche he received the complete transmissions of the *kLong chen snying thig* and the *rTsa rlung* precepts. In turn, A'dzom 'Brug pa became a *gter ston*, or discoverer of hidden treasure texts, having received visions directly from the incomparable 'Jigs med gLing pa (1730–98) when the former was thirty. Teaching at A'dzom sgar in eastern Tibet during summer and winter retreats,[5] A'dzom 'Brug pa became the master of many contemporary teachers of rDzogs chen. Among them was Norbu Rinpoche's paternal uncle, rTogs Idan O rgyan bs Tan 'dzin,[6] who was his first rDzogs chen teacher.

When he was eight years old, the sixteenth Karmapa,[7] and dPal spung Situ Rinpoche[8] both recognized Norbu Rinpoche to be the mind-incarnation[9] of Lho 'Brug Zhabs drung Rinpoche.[10] This latter master, the reincarnation of the illustrious 'Brug pa bKa' brgyud master, Padma dKar po (1527–92), was the actual historical founder of the state of Bhutan. Until the early twentieth century, the Zhabs drung Rinpoches were the Dharmarajas or temporal and spiritual rulers of Bhutan.

While yet a child, from rDzogs chen mKhan Rinpoche,[11] from his maternal uncle mKhyen brtse Yang srid Rinpoche,[12] and from his paternal uncle rTogs Idan O rgyan bs Tan 'dzin, Norbu Rinpoche received instruction in the *rDzogs chen gsang ba snying thig* and the *sNying thig Yab bzhi*. Meanwhile, from gNas rgyab mChog sprul Rinpoche,[13] he received the transmissions of the *rNying ma bka' ma*, the *kLong gsal rdo rje snying po*, and the *gNam chos* of Mi 'gyur rDo rje. From mKhan Rinpoche dPal Idan Tshul khrims (1906–) he received the transmissions from the *rGyud sde kun btus*, the famous Sa skya pa collection of tantric practices. And, in addition, he received many initiations and listened to many oral explanations[14] from the famous Ris med pa or nonsectarian masters of eastern Tibet.

From the time he was eight years old until he was twelve, he attended the college of sDe dge dbon stod slob grwa at sDe dge dgon chen

Monastery, where, with mKhen Rinpoche mKhyen rab Chos kyi 'od zer (1901–), he studied the thirteen basic texts[15] used in the standard academic curriculum designed by mKhan po gZhan dga'.[16] Norbu Rinpoche became especially expert in the *Abhisamayālaṅkāra*. In addition, with this same master he studied the great commentary to the *Kālacakra Tantra*,[17] the *Guhyagarbha Tantra*, the *Zab mo nang don* of Karmapa Rang byung rDo rje, the Medical Tantras,[18] Indian and Chinese astrology,[19] as well as receiving from him the initiations and transmissions of the *Sa skya'i sgrub thabs kun btus*.

From the age of eight until he was fourteen, at the college of sDe dge Ku se gSer ljongs bshad grwa, from mKhan Rinpoche Brag gyab Blos gros (1913–), he received instructions in the *Prajñā-pāramitā sutras*, the *Abhisamayālaṅkāra*, and three tantric texts: the *rDorje Gur*, the *Hevajra Tantra* and the *Samputa Tantra*.[20] By his tutor mChog sprul Rinpoche[21] he was instructed in the secular sciences.[22]

Also, from the age of eight until he was fourteen, having gone to rDzong gsar Monastery in eastern Tibet, he received teachings from the illustrious rDzong gsar mKhyen brtse Rinpoche[23] on the *Sa skya'i zab chos lam 'bras*, the quintessential doctrine of the Sa skya pa school, and in addition, on the three texts: *rGyud kyi spyi don rnam bzhag*, *Ijon shing chen mo*, and the *Hevajra Tantra*.[24] Then at the college of Khams bre bshad grwa, with mKhan Rinpoche Mi nyag Dam chos (1920–) he studied a basic text on logic, the *Tshad ma rig gter* of Sa skya Paṇḍita.

Then, in the meditation cave at Seng-chen gNam brag, he made a retreat with his uncle the rTogs ldan O rgyan bsTan 'dzin for the practices of Vajrapāṇi, Siṃhamukha, and White Tārā. At that time, the son of A'dzom 'Brug pa, 'Gyur med rDo rje (1895–), returned from Central Tibet, and staying with them, the latter bestowed the cycle of *rDo rje gro lod*, the *Klong chen snying thig*, and the cycle of the *dGongs pa zang thal* of Rig 'dzin rGod ldem 'Phru can.

When he was fourteen years old in 1951, he

received the initiations for Vajrayogini according to the Ngor pa and Tshar pa traditions of the Sa skya. Then his tutor advised him to seek out a woman living in the Kadari region who was the living embodiment of Vajrayogini herself and take initiation from her. This woman master, A yo mKha' 'gro rdo rje dPal sgron (1838–1953), was a direct disciple of the great 'Jam dbyangs mKhyen brtse dBang po and of Nyag bla Padma bDud 'dul, as well as being an elder contemporary of A 'dzom 'Brug pa. At this time she was 113 years old and had been in a dark retreat[25] for some fifty-six years. Norbu Rinpoche received from her transmissions for the *mKha' 'gro gsang 'dus*, the mind-treasure[26] of 'Jam dbyangs mKhyen brtse dBang po, and the *mKha' 'gro yang thig*, in which the principal practice is the dark retreat, as well as the *Klong chen snying thig*. She also bestowed upon him her own mind-treasures, including that for the Ḍākinī Siṃhamukha, the *mKha' 'gro dbang mo'i seng ge gdong ma'i zab thig*.

Then in 1954, he was invited to visit the People's Republic of China as a representative of Tibetan youth. From 1954 he was an instructor in Tibetan language at the Southwestern University of Minor Nationalities at Chengdu, Sichuan, China. While living in China, he met the famous Gangs dkar Rinpoche.[27] From the master he heard many explanations of the Six Doctrines of Nāropa,[28] Mahāmudrā, the *dKon mchog spyi 'dus*, as well as Tibetan medicine. During this time, Norbu Rinpoche also acquired proficiency in the Chinese and Mongolian languages.

When he was seventeen years old, returning to his home country of sDe dge following a vision received in dream, he came to meet his Root Master[29], Nyag bla Rinpoche Rig 'dzin Byang chub rDo rje (1826–1978), who lived in a remote valley to the east of sDe gde. Byang chub rDo rje Rinpoche hailed originally from the Nyag rong region on the borders of China. He was a disciple of A 'dzom 'Brug pa, of Nyag bla Padma dDud 'dul, and of Shar rdza Rinpoche[30], the famous Bonpo teacher of rDzogs chen who attained the Rainbow Body of

Light.[31] A practising physician, Byang chub rDo rje Rinpoche headed a commune called Nyag bla sGar in this remote valley; it was a totally self-supporting community consisting entirely of lay practitioners, yogins and yoginis. From this master, Norbu Rinpoche received initiation into, and transmission of, the essential teachings of rDzogs chen *Sems sde*, *Klong sde*, and *Man ngag gi sde*. More importantly, this master introduced him directly to the experience of rDzogs chen. He remained here for almost a year, often assisting Byang chub rDo rje Rinpoche in his medical practice and serving as his scribe and secretary. He also received transmissions from the master's son, Nyag sras 'Gyur med rDo rje.

After this, Norbu Rinpoche set out on a prolonged pilgrimage to Central Tibet, Nepal, India, and Bhutan. Returning to sDe dge, the land of his birth, he found that deteriorating political conditions had led to the eruption of violence. Fleeing first toward Central Tibet, he finally emerged safely in Sikkim as a refugee. From 1958 to 1960 he lived in Gangtok, Sikkim, employed as an author and editor of Tibetan text books for the Development Office, the Government of Sikkim. In 1960 when he was twenty-two years old, at the invitation of Professor Giuseppe Tucci, he went to Italy and resided for several years in Rome. During this time, from 1960 to 1964, he was a research associate at the Istituto Italiano per il Medio ed Estremo Oriente. Receiving a grant from the Rockefeller Foundation, he worked in close collaboration with Professor Tucci, and wrote two appendices to Professor Tucci's *Tibetan Folk Songs of Gyantse and Western Tibet* (Rome, 1966), as well as giving seminars at IsMEO on yoga, medicine, and astrology.

From 1964 to the present, Norbu Rinpoche has been a professor at the Istituto Orientale, University of Naples, where he teaches Tibetan language, Mongolian language, and Tibetan cultural history. Since then he has done extensive research into the historical origins of Tibetan culture, investigating little-known literary sources from the Bonpo tradition. In 1983, Norbu Rinpoche hosted the first International Convention on Tibetan Medicine held at Venice, Italy. Although still actively teaching at the university, for the past ten years Norbu Rinpoche has informally conducted teaching retreats in various countries, including Italy, France, England, Austria, Denmark, Norway, Finland, and since 1979, the United States. During these retreats, he gives practical instruction in rDzogs chen practices in a non-sectarian format, as well as teaching aspects of Tibetan culture, especially Yantra Yoga, Tibetan medicine and astrology. Moreover, under his guidance there has grown up, at first in Italy and now in several other countries, including the United States, what has come to be known as the Dzogchen Community.[32] This is an informal association of individuals who, while continuing to work at their usual occupations in society, share a common interest in pursuing and practising the teachings which Norbu Rinpoche continues to transmit.

The above information was largely extracted by John Reynolds from a biography in Tibetan appended to Professor Norbu's *gZi yi Phreng ba* (Dharmsala: Library of Tibetan Works and Archives, 1982).

The Lóndé series: the four syllables of the Lóndé: the dórjéi ciglam, or 'vajra syllable way'

The four syllables, representing four words, provide a summary of how one practises the Lóndé.

'Ă' is the first syllable, and it represents the word 'gyeva medba', which means 'unborn', referring to the state of 'midogba', which is 'without thought'. The essential state of voidness, Šūnyatā, is unborn. The mind of the practitioner is said to return continually to contemplation, in the same way that a dove, used by sailors to test for the presence of land when they are out at sea, returns right away to the ship when it finds nothing there.

'Ho' is the second syllable, and it represents the word 'gàgba medba', which means 'without interruption'. Although one knows that all thoughts are void, yet there is still nevertheless the continual arising of thought. When we explain the Xì, or Base, the primordial state of the individual, (see p. 56), it is explained that its Essence is void, but its Nature is to manifest continually, without interruption. The syllable Ho is a symbol of the way the practitioner maintains uninterrupted presence of awareness in contemplation, applying the methods of the four Dá (p. 80). So the practitioner is said to be like an archer, who must unite Body, Voice, or energy, and Mind, in what he is doing when he shoots, if his arrow is to hit the mark. The practitioners uninterrupted awareness must be kept present in the same way.

'Ha' is the third syllable, and it stands for the word 'migyùrva', which means 'unchanging', 'immutable', and is a symbol of the fact that the primordial state, into which one enters in contemplation, is the fundamental, immutable condition of every individual, that has always already existed right from the beginning, and does not need to be created. This state has been obstructed only by the arising of impure vision as a result of attachment and negative causes. When the practitioner, by means of the practice, overcomes these obstacles, re-entering the primordial state, he or she becomes like a new born baby, not in the sense of being babyish, but in that the practitioner's awareness becomes as nakedly clear as that of a new born baby, who looks at the world in each moment without judgment.

'Ye' is the fourth and last letter, and various sources in various ancient texts give different derivations for it. In some texts it is considered that the syllable is 'Ye', but in others it is regarded as being 'Eh', which is a little like an 'ah' with an E symbol over it. It is not easy to be certain which is the correct interpretation, but it is more likely to be 'Ye', as in 'Yeshes', which means wisdom. 'Ye' in Tibetan means 'from the beginning', or 'originally'. But one cannot be sure that this 'Ye' is a Tibetan syllable. It could be a syllable of the language of Urgyán, or Odiyana, in which case it is more likely to be 'eh' than 'Ye'. However, whatever its derivation, the syllable is a symbol of the word 'nàcog', which means 'variety', in the sense of the infinite variety of the possibility of manifestations in one's karmic vision, and the way in which the practitioner effortlessly integrates with whatever of these infinite variety of possibilities arises to him, entering into contemplation and continuing in it through all the various aspects of his daily life. In this the practitioner is said to be like a water mill, that just keeps on turning as long as the water keeps flowing, relaxedly, and all of itself. Effortlessly one mixes all one's actions of Body, Voice, and Mind, and everything that arises as one's karmic vision, with the state of contemplation.

Notes

1 My birth, early life and education; and how I came to meet my principal master

1 See Appendix 2, p. 153 for a more detailed biography of the author.

2 An introductory perspective; the Zógqen teachings and the culture of Tibet

1 For a full treatment of the significance of Bŏn in Tibetan culture, see the author's *The Necklace of Gzi, A Cultural History of Tibet*, published by the Information Office of His Holiness the Dalai Lama, Dharmsala, India, 1980, in English.

3 How my master Jyăṅqub Dórjé showed me the real meaning of Direct Introduction

1 The Tibetan calendar is arranged in a lunar calendar whose cycle begins with the New Moon in February. New Moon is from then on always the first of the month, and Full Moon is always on the 15th. From a tantric point of view, the period of the waxing moon favours method, and therefore Heruka practices are done during this phase, within which the 10th day of the month is considered particularly auspicious, and is known as Padmasambhava's day, because the great master carried out very many actions on that day. The period of the waning moon, on the other hand, favours energy, and Dākinī practices are thus carried out during this phase of the moon, with the 25th day known as Dākinī day, being particularly auspicious. The 8th day of the month is dedicated to Tārā and to Mahākāla, while the 29th is dedicated to the Guardians

of the teachings in general. The days of the week are the same as those in the Western calendar.

2 Bărdo: in general use this term refers to the intermediate state that follows the death of the physical body, and precedes the next rebirth. More precisely there are six Bărdos.

3 The Jyăñqubsem Gómba', or 'Meditation on Bodhicitta', recently translated into English by the author and Dr Kennard Lipman. To be published shortly be Shambhala Publications, Boston, Autumn 1986, with the title: 'Primordial Experience'.

4 Bodhisattva: one who is committed to total realization for the benefit of all other beings.

5 Hidden texts or objects, and teachings revealed through the great mental clarity of certain masters. See commentary to plate 5.

4 Zógqen in relation to the various levels of the Buddhist path

1 See the author's *Dzogchen and Zen*, Zhang Zhung Editions, Oakland, California, 1984, for a full treatment of this topic. Essentially the difference is this: While the practitioner of Zen aims to realize an empty state of mind free of concepts about reality (Tib: Mitogba), the practitioner of Zógqen aims to go beyond this void state of mind to realize a state of pure primordial presence (Tib: Rigba) in which a total reintegration of the energy that is the continual manifest function of the void can be accomplished.

2 He also taught those Bŏn practitioners who approached him for teaching.

5 With my two uncles who were Zógqen masters

1 See the author's: *A Journey into the Culture of Tibetan Nomads*, Shan-Shung Editions, Merigar 58031 Arcidosso G.R. Italy, 1983. At present only available in Tibetan, with English introduction.

2 See: *Women of Wisdom*, Tsultrim Allione, Routledge & Kegan Paul, London, 1984.

3 See: *The Life of Marpa the Translator*, tr. Nalanda/Trungpa, Prajña Press, Boulder, 1983 and *The*

100,000 Songs of Milarepa, tr. Garma C. Chang, Shambhala, Boulder, 1977 (2 vols).

6 The Base

1 All teachings have their own particular Base, Path and Fruit which determine the specific characteristics of the teaching. How it considers the fundamental condition of the individual (Base), what spiritual practice must be done (Path), and what state is ideally to be attained (Fruit). What is presented here is the Base, Path, and Fruit of Zógqen.

2 The Song of the Vajra comes from the 'Ñidá Kajyór', the 'Union of the Solar and Lunar' tantra. It is also the principal mantra of the 'Bărdo Tosdrŏl', known in the West as the 'Tibetan Book of the Dead', and its syllables, in its original form, are in the language of Urgyán, the language of the Ḍākinīs. The song is not a prayer, nor does the practice of it involve a visualization; rather it is a form of contemplation, in which the practitioner integrates the mind with the level of energy through the sound of the song as he or she chants it. Thus, in practice, its meaning is not as important as its sound.

3 'Kam': (Tibetan): Essence of the elements: 'jyùñva': elements.

4 See: *Death, Intermediate State and Rebirth in Tibetan Buddhism*, Lati Rinbochay and Jeffrey Hopkins, Rider, London, 1979; and also, the author's Italian translation of the Tibetan Book of the Dead: *Il Libro Tibetano dei Morti* Namkhai Norbu, Newton Compton, Editori, Rome, 1983.

7 The Path

1 In this analogy, the clarity, purity and limpidity of the mirror represent the Absolute, while the reflections arising in the mirror – which have no concrete substance – represent the illusoriness of the Relative. Yet Relative and Absolute are shown to be inter-dependent and mutually arising because a mirror cannot exist without reflections, nor reflections without a mirror.

2 See: *The Life and Teaching of Naropa*, H. V. Guenther, Oxford, 1963.

3 Note that there do exist also both internal and external Ǹòndrò in the Mannagdé, but that they are not compulsory preliminaries.

4 *Editor's note*: see *Clear Light of Bliss. Mahāmudrā in Vajrayāna Buddhism*, Geshe Kelsang Gyatso, Wisdom Publications, London, 1982, p.126. 'The practice with the action seal 'karmamudrā' refers to the meditation with an actual consort. In order to practise with the action seal here at the completion stage you must already be familiar with causing your winds (subtle energies) to enter, abide, and dissolve in the central channel through the force of meditation. A person who cannot control the winds in this way through meditation cannot possibly do so through copulation. A lay practitioner who is currently unable to transform sexual activity into the path in this way should generate strong aspiration and motivation to be able to do so in future.'

5 See the author's, *Yantra Yoga. The Yoga of Movement*, Shanshung Editions (Dzogchen Community Publishing), Naples, 1982. At present (1985) available only in Tibetan with English introduction, but translation into European languages is now nearing completion. The book contains the root text of Vairocana, and a commentary by Namkhai Norbu.

6 Hūṃkara was both a teacher and disciple of Padmasambhava.

7 See: *The Divine Madman: The Sublime Life and Songs of Drukpa Kunley*, translated by Keith Dowman, Rider, London, 1980.

8 This short biography of Ayu Kàdro, by the author is now published in *Women of Wisdom*, ed. Tsultrim Allione, Routledge & Kegan Paul, London, 1984.

Appendix 1   The mirror

1 The *Kun-byed rgyal-po*, when translated means 'The King which creates everything', and is the principal *tantra* of the *Sems-de* or Series of the Mind, one of the three series of the written *rDzog-chen* teachings.

2 The Six states of existence (*rigs-drug*) are the six principal dimensions of karmic vision, each one

Il Libro Tibetano Dei Morti, translation into Italian of The Tibetan Book of the Dead, published by Newton Compton Editori, Rome, Italy, 1983.

Primordial Experience: Mañjuśrimitra's Treatise on the Meaning of Bodhicitta in rDzogsChen, Namkhai Norbu with Kennard Lipman in collaboration with Barry Simmons, translation from Tibetan into English, to be published by Shambhala Publications, Boston, Autumn 1986.

In: *Women of Wisdom*, by Tsultrim Allione, published by Routledge & Kegan Paul, London, 1984, 'The Biography of A-Yu Khadro, Dorje Paldron', written by Namkhai Norbu.

Yantra Yoga: The Yoga of Movement. Root text by Vairocana in Tibetan, with extensive commentary, in Tibetan, introduction in English, published by Shang-Shung Edizioni, Merigar, 58031 Arcidosso, G.R., Italy. (Translation into European languages in progress 1985.)

Zer-Nga: The Five Principal Points. A Dzogchen Upadesha Practice, published by Shang-Shung Editions, London, 1985. (14D Chesterton Road, London, W10, England.)

Information about retreats conducted by Namkhai Norbu Rinpoche in various parts of the world, and transcripts of tapes of some of his past retreats are available from:
Comunità Dzogchen: Merigar, 58031 Arcidosso, G.R., Italy.
Dzogchen Community, West Coast, 4097 Shafter Avenue, Oakland, California 94609, USA.
Dzogchen Community, RFDI, Box 221, Conway, Massachusetts, 01341, USA.
Dzogchen Community UK, 14D Chesterton Road, London, W10, England.
Dzogchen Community, 8 Rue Bernard de Clairvaux, 75003, Paris, France.

Index

PENGUIN

ARKANA

NEW AGE BOOKS FOR MIND, BODY & SPIRIT

With over 200 titles currently in print, Arkana is the leading name in quality books for mind, body and spirit. Arkana encompasses the spirituality of both East and West, ancient and new. A vast range of interests is covered, including Psychology and Transformation, Health, Science and Mysticism, Women's Spirituality, Zen, Western Traditions and Astrology.

If you would like a catalogue of Arkana books, please write to:

Sales Dept. – Arkana
Penguin Books USA Inc.
375 Hudson Street
New York, NY 10014

Arkana Marketing Department
Penguin Books Ltd
27 Wrights Lane
London W8 5TZ

PENGUIN
ARKANA

NEW AGE BOOKS FOR MIND, BODY & SPIRIT

A SELECTION OF TITLES

The Dreambody in Relationships   Arnold Mindell

All of us communicate on several levels at once, and Mindell shows how much of our silent language conflicts with overt behaviour. He argues that bringing all the hidden parts of ourselves to awareness as they affect us is important for the well-being not only of our relationships but also of the community – indeed, the world – in which we live.

Buddhism   Geshe Kelsang Gyatso

Tibetan Buddhism has in many respects preserved the original teachings of the Buddha. Here they are presented with great wisdom and the paths towards liberation and enlightenment mapped out with painstaking care. For those seeking spiritual awakening, peace and serenity, this excellent book will open up a world of new possiblities.

Be As You Are   Sri Ramana Maharshi

'The ultimate truth is so simple.' This is the message of Sri Ramana Maharshi, one of India's most revered spiritual masters whose teachings, forty years after his death, are speaking to growing audiences worldwide. 'That sense of presence, of the direct communication of the truth so far as it can be put into words, is there on every page' – *Parabola*

In Search of the Miraculous: Fragments of an Unknown Teaching   P. D. Ouspensky

Ouspensky's renowned, vivid and characteristically honest account of his work with Gurdjieff from 1915–18. 'Undoubtedly a *tour de force*. To put entirely new and very complex cosmology and psychology into fewer than 400 pages, and to do this with a simplicity and vividness that makes the book accessible to any educated reader, is in itself something of an achievement' – *The Times Literary Supplement*

PENGUIN

ARKANA

NEW AGE BOOKS FOR MIND, BODY & SPIRIT

A SELECTION OF TITLES

When the Iron Eagle Flies: Buddhism for the West Ayya Khema

'One of humanity's greatest jewels'. Such are the teachings of the Buddha, unfolded here simply, free of jargon. This practical guide to meaning through awareness contains a wealth of exercises and advice to help the reader on his or her way.

The Second Ring of Power Carlos Casteneda

Carlos Castaneda's journey into the world of sorcery has captivated millions. In this fifth book, he introduces the reader to Dona Soledad, whose mission is to test Castaneda by a series of terrifying tricks. Thus Castaneda is initiated into experiences so intense, so profoundly disturbing, as to be an assault on reason and on every preconceived notion of life...

Dialogues with Scientists and Sages: The Search for Unity
Renée Weber

In their own words, contemporary scientists and mystics – from the Dalai Lama to Stephen Hawking – share with us their richly diverse views on space, time, matter, energy, life, consciousness, creation and our place in the scheme of things. Through the immediacy of verbatim dialogue, we encounter scientists who endorse mysticism, and those who oppose it; mystics who dismiss science, and those who embrace it.

The Way of the Sufi Idries Shah

Sufism, the mystical aspect of Islam, has had a dynamic and lasting effect on the literature of that religion. Its teachings, often elusive and subtle, aim at the perfecting and completing of the human mind. In this wide-ranging anthology of Sufi writing Idries Shah offers a broad selection of poetry, contemplations, letters, lectures and teaching stories that together form an illuminating introduction to this unique body of thought.